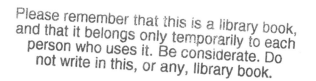

SCHOOLS AND SOCIAL JUSTICE

R.W. CONNELL

Temple University Press
Philadelphia

Temple University Press, Philadelphia 19122

Copyright © 1993 by R.W. Connell

Published 1993

Printed in the United States of America

This book is printed on acid-free paper.

ISBN 1-56639-137-7 (cloth)

ISBN 1-56639-138-5 (paper)

Cataloging-in-Publication Data available from the Library of Congress.

Preface

This book is an academic's reflections on troubling issues about schools. Academics are, almost by definition, people who have been well served by the education system as it now is. They should never forget that there are many others who have been much worse served. This book asks why, and what can be done about it.

My starting-point is research on Australian schools, particularly a recent project on disadvantaged schools. But I am writing equally for readers in other countries. Half of the chapters began as addresses to audiences in Canada, the United States and Britain. They draw on my experience in universities in those three countries, as researcher and teacher, and on a continuing interest in their school systems. These systems not only have common origins, they are increasingly bound together by global communications, international agencies and multinational corporations. I think it is extremely important for democratic forces in different countries to share ideas and experiences; the issues they face are genuinely global in scale.

All intellectual work is collective work, in an important sense. Though I have written this text, it is deeply indebted to co-workers: especially Viv White and Ken Johnston, and the many other people who worked on the Disadvantaged Schools Program study; and Dean Ashenden, Sandra Kessler and Gary Dowsett, my co-workers on the earlier research that led to *Making the Difference* and *Teachers' Work*. I have learned from their example as well as their ideas.

Part of the social process of research is being encouraged to grapple with particular issues by invitations (some being the kind you can't refuse) to speak or write on the subject. I would like to acknowledge the following groups who have coerced me into doing work drawn on in this book: organizers of the National Conference on Poverty and Education, Adelaide 1989, for the invitation to speak on 'Poverty, education, and strategy for educational reform;' the Australian Council of Social Service, for the invitation to speak to their National Congress, Melbourne 1989, on 'Schools and social justice;' the Ministerial Consultative Council on Curriculum, Queensland, and the Australian Curriculum Studies Association, for the invitation to speak at their Curriculum Directions for the 1990s conference, Brisbane 1990, on 'Curriculum and social justice;' organizers of the Poverty and Education Summit Conference, Sydney 1990, for the invitation to speak on 'Poverty and empowerment;' the Toronto Board of Education, for the invitation to speak at their conference on Assessing Student Performance Productively, Toronto 1991, on 'Poverty and educational measurement;' organizers of the International Conference on Sociology of Education, Westhill 1992, for the invitation to speak on 'Citizenship, social justice, and curriculum;' the School of Education, University of Pittsburgh, for the invitation to deliver the 1992 Paul Masoner International Education Lecture, on 'Education and poverty;' the Centre for Educational Research and Innovation, Organisation for Economic Co-operation and Development, for the invitation to speak at their seminar on trends in educational research and development, Washington 1992, on 'New approaches to research for educational renovation.' This is more than a formal acknowledgment; the occasions, and the discussions around them, were important in shaping the ideas that follow. Organizing conferences is an important and under-valued form of intellectual work.

I am grateful to the Australian Council for Educational Research for permission to reproduce the graph in Figure 1, which appeared in T. Williams, *Participation in Education*, Melbourne, ACER, 1987, and for permission to reproduce in Chapter 5 material that originally appeared in my article The Workforce of Reform in *Australian Journal of Education*, 1991, vol. 35 no. 3; to Prof. Len Barton, editor of *British Jour-*

nal of Sociology of Education, for permission to reproduce in Chapter 7 material originally published as R.W. Connell, V.M. White and K.M. Johnston, 'An Experiment in Justice: the Disadvantaged Schools Program and the Question of Poverty, 1974–1990', *BJSE*, 1992, vol. 13 no. 4; to the Organisation for Economic Co-operation and Development, for permission to reproduce material in Chapter 8 originally presented as a paper at an OECD conference.

For all this support, none of this reflection would have occurred without a basis of progressive practice in the schools. Most of the ideas in this book are drawn from the work and words of activists in public schools, and research performs a useful function if it does no more than circulate their experiences. I would like to dedicate this book to the teachers who have dedicated their lives to the service of working-class, poor and disadvantaged children.

Santa Cruz, March 1993   *Bob Connell*

Contents

PART ONE: PRINCIPLES

Chapter One

Social Justice In Education

Why Does This Issue Matter?

To many people, questions about education and questions about social justice belong in separate baskets. Education concerns schools, colleges and universities, whose business is to pass knowledge on to the next generation. Social justice is about income, employment, pensions or physical assets like housing. Governments have separate departments for them, and so should our minds. The schools have no business getting mixed up with welfare; their job is to teach.

It is easier to believe in this separation if you are yourself well-paid and well-educated. People who are poor and who have been ill-educated have been raising questions for a long time about the connection: about who the education system is actually serving, and why it seems closed or indifferent to the likes of them.

I think these questions are valid and important, not only for the disadvantaged. There are, it seems to me, three key reasons why the issue of social justice matters for everyone connected with the school system — teachers, parents, pupils and administrators alike.

(1) The education system is a major public asset. It is one of the largest industries in any modern economy; it is one of the largest public undertakings. In Canada, for instance, public

expenditure on education runs at $54,170,406,000 per year (1991–92); not a cottage industry.[1] In many communities, especially working-class communities, the public schools are the largest institutions around, and the most important centres of neighbourhood activity.

Teachers, harassed with demands and fighting budget cuts, and seeing little immediate return from much of their work (since education is a slow, long-term process), easily forget this. But schools *are* major social institutions, they have weight in the world. It is not just election-year rhetoric to say that it does matter to society as a whole how schools work, and how well they work.

Given the scale of this public asset, who gets its benefits is a serious question. And there is an immediate reason for asking about social justice. Educational institutions themselves have a shape that shows an unequal distribution of benefits. Western-style education systems have a pyramid shape. As you get closer to the top of the system, fewer and fewer people are there to get the benefits.

(The pyramid narrows sooner in poor countries, where most people are lucky to get a full elementary education. In the richest countries, the institutional narrowing is most noticeable at the tertiary level. Thus if we look at education on a world scale, there is a pyramid of pyramids.)

This immediately means an unequal distribution of the resource represented by formal education. Some idea of the scale of this inequality is given by adding up the public costs of educating young people who leave the system at different levels. An Australian comparison showed the (current-dollar) public expenditure on the schooling of a youth who left high school after year 9 to be $33 600, while the amount spent on an age-mate who left after a four-year chemistry degree was $79 800.[2] These are only indicative figures, but they do point to the order of magnitude involved.

Who gets to the upper levels of the pyramid? Social researchers have compiled abundant evidence about this, documenting how retention rates in secondary schooling, access to higher education, or other educational 'outcomes,' differ between social classes, regions, ethnic groups. Figure 1 shows one example, from literally hundreds that could be shown. The contours vary from place to place, and from time to time, but the underlying fact remains. There is massive evidence of inequalities in chances of benefiting from the upper levels of education, depending on social background.

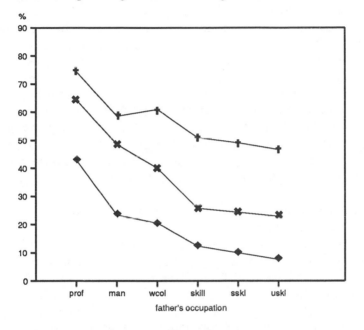

Figure 1.

Social class (index: father's occupation) and some educational outcomes: entry to post-secondary courses, completion of year 12 secondary schooling, and entry to higher education in Australia. Source: T. Williams, *Participation in Education*, Melbourne, ACER, 1987.

So, despite the great expansion of the education system in the last two generations, the results have been lopsided in terms of social access. It is common, in studies like those in Figure 1, for children from the most advantaged groups to show two to four times the rate of entry to higher education that children of least advantaged groups have. To give a Canadian example: in an analysis of 1981 Ontario census data, Paul Anisef found that the percentage of young women (aged 18–21) who were at university ranged from 44.4 per cent for those whose fathers had a university degree, down to 10.3 per cent for those whose fathers had only elementary education; for young men the corresponding figures were 39.9 per cent and 8.7 per cent.[3] That is the scale of inequality, even in large aggregate figures. The position for particular minorities, such as Australian Aboriginal children, is worse.

(2) Not only is the education system a major public asset now — it is likely to become more important in future.

Many economic and social commentators have argued that education is becoming more important as an asset in the late twentieth century. Organized knowledge has certainly become a more important component of the production system. I am writing this in California not far from 'Silicon Valley,' the centre of the U.S. computer industry. Information industries, based on the education system and its capacities for research and training, are now key determinants of economic growth or decline.

So it is not accidental that we hear so much talk at present about the economic uses of education: labour productivity, skills formation, support for advanced technology. But the point is broader than simply technical education. More and more jobs in all kinds of fields have become credentialed. It is a long time since you could become a doctor without having a medical degree, and that 'professional' model is spreading. As new degree programs multiply in human kinetics, leisure studies, business administration, etc., it becomes more and more difficult to get a job as a sports coach, camp administrator, company manager, etc., without the corresponding degree. The education system becomes more and more important as a gatekeeper.

The education system, then, not only distributes current social assets. It also shapes the kind of society that is coming into being. Whether our future society is a just one depends, in part, on the use we make of the education system now.

(3) My third point is about what it is to *educate*. Teaching has been described as a 'moral trade,' and I think this is profoundly true. Teaching and learning, as social practices, *always* involve questions about purposes and criteria for action (whether those purposes are shared or not), about the applica-

tion of resources (including authority and knowledge), and about responsibility and the consequences of action.

These issues cannot be evaded. If you try to dodge them by going into value-neutral technocratic mode and teaching only 'information' (an attitude common, for instance, in natural science and mathematics teaching), then *by default* you are teaching lessons of moral indifference and lack of responsibility. (These are chickens that came home to roost in high-tech environmental disasters.) As we all know, the 'hidden curriculum' contained in the way schools treat their pupils is as powerful an educational force as the official curriculum.

The moral quality of education is inevitably affected by the moral character of educational institutions. If the school system is dealing unjustly with some of its pupils, they are not the only ones to suffer. *The quality of education for all the others is degraded.*

I would like to shout this from the rooftops every time I hear another argument for 'gifted and talented' programs, for tougher 'standards' and stricter selection, for streaming or tracking, for merit awards and opportunity schools and honours programs — in short, for any of the hundred and one affronts to equal provision of education. An education that privileges one child over another is giving the privileged child a corrupted education, even as it gives him or her a social or economic advantage.

The issue of social justice is not an add-on. It is fundamental to what good education is about.

The Meaning Of Justice In Education

Questions about 'education and justice' are certainly not new. In the Western philosophical tradition the first great treatise on education, Plato's *Republic*, was also the first great treatise on justice. In neo-Confucian China, the legitimacy of the scholar-official system of government flowed from open selection to the elite by literary exams.

But we would hardly rest our current ideal of education on elite concepts like Plato's guardians or Confucian mandarins. In modern discussions the issue of 'education and justice' has been framed another way. Debates centre on the service provided to the whole population by a mass education system, and are posed as questions of distributive justice.

Questions of 'distributive justice' are questions about who gets what — particularly, who gets how much of some social good. The most familiar 'social good' is money, and the distribution of wealth and income is much debated. For instance, recent research estimates that the richest 5 per cent of Australians own about 50 per cent of the country's total private wealth.[4] The position in other Western countries is similar.

Such figures always raise arguments as to whether too much wealth is concentrated in too few hands. That is the classic form of an argument about distributive justice: do some people have too much, others too little? As the philosopher Michael Walzer shows, distributive questions can be raised about a whole series of 'social goods:' money, welfare, office, leisure, love, grace, recognition — and education.[5]

In what follows, I use the term 'justice' in the sense of Walzer and of John Rawls' famous book *A Theory of Justice*, as a question of fairness in distribution for which the normal criterion is equality.[6] There is another common usage of 'justice' that refers to getting what one deserves — for instance in 'criminal justice,' or 'wage justice.' For the case of social justice in education, the two usages converge. 'Deserts' of individuals may differ markedly, as the criminal law presumes. But it is difficult to see how a whole social group can *deserve* either more or less education than another social group; so this conception too points to equality.

But there is a risk, in emphasising equality in distribution, that it will be seen only as a matter of individual rights. So we should take note of the other tradition of thought about justice, descending from Plato, that emphasises balance and harmony in the social life we all share. Individual equality is the condition, not the goal, of a just *social order*. The quality of our collective life is central to the argument. Seventy years ago L.T. Hobhouse (the first professor of sociology in England) put it clearly in a book called *The Elements of Social Justice*:

> Acts and institutions are good not because they suit a majority, but because they make the nearest possible approach to a good shared by every single person whom they affect.[7]

16

Over the last 150 years or so, in 'Western' and Western-influenced societies, questions of justice in education have mainly been about access to formal schooling and certification. The 150 year span is, roughly, the life-span of state-funded, bureaucratically-controlled mass elementary school systems. Mass elementary schooling has everywhere coexisted with a much more selective (sometimes private) provision of secondary and higher education.

Out of this history came two great questions of distributive justice. The first was about providing elementary education for the whole population. This issue is now settled in countries like Canada and Australia, far from settled in countries like India.

The second was about fair access to the selective upper levels of formal education. Secondary schooling was the focus of this issue in industrialised countries for most of this century. Now higher education increasingly is the focus. We see debates hotting up about university enrollments and overall funding — that is, about how much access there shall be. We see debates about university fees and rich students buying university places — that is, about who shall have access.

These distributive questions underlie the two great enterprises in educational justice that have been undertaken in the last generation. On a world scale, justice is pursued by the creation of universal elementary school systems, and by campaigns for universal literacy, in poor countries. This broadens the base of the educational pyramid.

In affluent countries like the United States, Britain and Australia, attempts are made to establish 'equal opportunity' in education via scholarships, compensatory education, desegregation, affirmative action, Assisted Places schemes, etc.

Broadly, both of these enterprises take the content and form of education for granted. The 'social good' they seek to distribute is the educational service provided by bureaucratically-controlled mass schooling systems, of the type created in Europe and North America in the mid 19th century.

The debates about *justice* are about who gets how much of this service (as measured, for instance, by that staple variable in survey research, 'years of education'). Compensatory and equal opportunity programs are essentially designed to make sure it is more widely delivered. *What* the service is, is debated in a separate theatre altogether — the theatre of curriculum theory, teaching method and the psychology of learning.

This split is revealed when education authorities make explicit statements about their efforts on behalf of the disadvantaged. Australia provides particularly interesting examples. In the late 1980s the Australian Labor Party, faced with an increasingly disillusioned rank-and-file, tried to formulate a 'social justice' policy. Education was included in the resulting policy statements, which are among the clearest recent formulations of the issue of justice in Western education policy.[8] A careful look at these documents shows that they remain within the distributive framework.

Here, for instance, is the 'overall objective' of equity policy in higher education as formulated in *A Fair Chance For All*, issued in 1990:

> To ensure that Australians from all groups in society have the opportunity to participate successfully in higher education. This will be achieved by changing the balance of the student population to reflect more closely the composition of society as a whole.[9]

Such statements raise scarcely any questions about what *kind* of education is being provided. That is taken for granted. The issue they address is who gets how much of the familiar product.

The underlying weakness of this approach to educational justice is its indifference to the nature of education itself. For education is a social process in which the 'how much' cannot be separated from the 'what.' There is an inescapable link between distribution and content.

I learnt about the connection between content and distribution during the collaborative research for *Making the Difference*.[10] Starting from the idea that the unequal distribution of education between social classes had to do with differences between working-class and ruling-class families, we found this was so only because they had different relationships with a particular kind of curriculum. The hegemonic curriculum in Australian high schools has a class history embedded in it, and has always operated to include and exclude students on class lines.

Broadly similar conclusions have been widespread in the sociology of education over the last two or three decades. Researchers in France, the United States, Britain, Canada and Australia all found the relationship between school knowledge and the production of social inequality to be a key issue.[11]

A crucial policy conclusion follows. Justice cannot be achieved by distributing the same amount of a standard good to children of all social classes. Education is a process operating through relationships, which *cannot* be neutralized or obliterated to allow equal distribution of the social good at their core. That 'good' means different things to ruling-class and working-class children, and will do different things for them (or to them).

This requires us to re-think the issue of justice in education *around the issue of curriculum*. Questions of distributive justice remain important; nothing I have said up to this point needs to be retracted. But distributive justice is an *incomplete* way of understanding educational issues. We need another kind of concept, which I will call *curricular justice*.

In Chapter 4 I will attempt to state a concept of curricular justice in enough detail to make it useful for practical purposes. But first let us look at the starkest issue of social justice in education, the question of poverty.

Chapter Two

Poverty And Compensatory Education

Poverty takes three main forms across the world. What we might call *Poverty 1*, the widest spread, is the poverty of third-world rural communities, brought into the world capitalist economy but deprived of most of its benefits, who live on some combination of subsistence agriculture, cash-cropping, and irregular wage labour.[1] Educational questions here centre on adult literacy and on the impact of the elementary school as a social form.

Poverty 2 is the poverty of urban populations in low-wage economies, a situation that includes such massive agglomerations as Mexico and Calcutta. Educational questions here centre on the effects of explosive urban growth and migration from impoverished countryside to unregulated urban market.

Poverty 3 is the poverty that results from inequality in high-wage economies, such as in Canada, the United States and Australia. This is the case I will focus on.

There are of course economic links between the three situations, and educational lessons to be passed on. Thus the ideas of Paulo Freire,[2] working in the context of Poverty 1 in Latin America, have inspired teachers working in high-wage economies with Poverty 3. But it is also important to recognize differences. The idea of a culture of poverty, worked out by anthropologists such as Oscar Lewis in the context of Poverty 2,[3] proved misleading, even damaging, when applied uncritically to Poverty 3.

People in poverty in high-wage economies (Poverty 3) are usually counted by drawing a 'poverty line' across the total income distribution, at a point fixed by some (distinctly out-dated) calculations about minimum food needs for families. By the austere U.S. government poverty line, the United States counted 12 million children in poverty in 1989.[4] Extrapolating from that figure the numbers of children in Poverty 3 internationally may be of the order of 35 million.

Education And Disadvantage

These children are the group whose educational needs have been addressed by means of compensatory education. Compensatory education programs were set up in a number of rich capitalist countries in the 1960s and 1970s, including the U.S., Britain, the Netherlands, and Australia.

Details of these programs vary from country to country, but they have some design elements in common. They are targeted, addressed to a minority of children (in Australia, about 15 per cent). The children are selected by a poverty-line calculation of some kind. The programs are intended to compensate for disadvantage by enriching the children's educational environment. They do this by grafting something on to the existing education system, and often are administered separately from conventional school funding.

These programs were introduced as it became clear that the vast expansion of education systems through the twentieth century had failed to deliver social justice. It is worth recalling that earlier in this century, most education systems were deliberately stratified. They were segregated by race, by gender and by class, streamed between academic and technical institutions, divided between public and private, Protestant and Catholic.

Early twentieth century education systems were inegalitarian in every pore; they exuded selectiveness and exclusion. (That was what Dewey contested in *Democracy and Education*,[5] a book whose radicalism is mostly forgotten.) Long struggles followed to desegregate schools, to establish comprehensive high schools, and to open universities.

Important successes were won. There is no doubt that school systems now are less strikingly unequal than they were two generations ago. Most decisively, these struggles for social justice established the principle of formally equal access to schooling for all children. This was crystallised in 1959 in the UN *Declaration of the Rights of the Child.*

But this turned out to be, at best, half a victory. Formally equal education still worked worse for disadvantaged children. Evidence accumulated that poor children did worse than rich children on tests and examinations, were more likely to be held back, dropped out earlier, were much less likely to enter university. A sample of this evidence was given in Chapter 1. Statistically speaking, the best advice we can give to a poor child keen to get ahead through education is to choose richer parents.

Since re-allocating parents is not within the constitutional power of most ministers of education,[6] the policy response was to do the next best thing: substitute through official agencies for the assets the children were not getting via their actual parents. Thus compensatory education was born.

It was born in a context of social welfare reform, and this affected its design. In the U.S. the 'rediscovery of poverty' and the political strategies of the Kennedy/Johnson administration in the 1960s led to the War on Poverty. The War on Poverty's main strategists were welfare economists, and its main success was the reduction of poverty among the elderly — not among children.

Education was brought into the welfare picture through the correlation between lower levels of education on the one side, higher rates of unemployment and lower wages on the other. The idea of a self-sustaining cycle of poverty emerged, where low aspirations and poor support for children led to low educational achievement. This in turn was supposed to lead to labour market failure and poverty in the next generation. Compensatory education was seen as a means to break into this cycle and derail the inheritance of poverty.[7]

A False Geography Of The Problem

The circumstances of this birth, and the political circumstances surrounding the survival of compensatory programs, have created a false geography of the problem. By this I mean a set of assumptions that continue to direct public policy making and public debate about the issues, but which are known to be wrong. I will be summary about them, as I wish to get on to more constructive argument, but they have to be noted because so many people work from this conceptual map.

(1) The belief that *educational inequality is a problem about a disadvantaged minority* — say, 15 per cent of the school population. This quietly presumes that the other 85 per cent, the 'mainstream,' are all on the same footing.

But this is not what the statistics of dropout or of university entry show. Another minority is highly *advantaged*. And in the 'middle' there is still a gradient of advantage and disadvantage. Poor children suffer the most severe effects of the larger pattern, they are not outside it.[8]

(2) The belief that *the poor are culturally different from the majority*. The American 'culture of poverty' thesis had its head cut off in the 1960s, in the controversy over the Moynihan Report. It then grew ten new ones: welfare dependency, underclass behavior, and so on.[9]

Several of these heads grew in education. A remarkable amount of research still goes looking for evidence of the psychological, attitudinal or cultural distinctiveness of poor children. With little success. The bulk of evidence actually demonstrates the cultural *similarity* between the poorest groups and the less poor.[10]

(3) The belief that *educational reform is a technical problem* which requires above all the application of research-based expertise. After twenty or thirty years of experts not finding top-down solutions, the search is still on for a technical fix. Thus the 'Effective Schools' movement; and on a wider front, the neoconservative attempt at school reform via national testing and twentieth-century versions of Payment by Results.[11]

In Boston one can view the astonishing sight of a whole disadvantaged school system taken over by a university — as if sheer management expertise could overcome the appalling effects of community poverty. (I do think there is a role for educational researchers — but not this one! See Chapter 8.)

The effect of this false geography of the problem has been to locate the problem in the heads of the poor or the errors of the specific schools serving them. The virtues of the educational mainstream are taken for granted. But this comfortable view has not been possible for many of the teachers in disadvantaged schools.

Conventional subject-matter and texts, traditional teaching methods and assessment, turn out to be sources of systematic difficulty. To teach well in such schools requires a shift in curriculum and pedagogy — a shift that is documented in the Disadvantaged Schools Program in Australia as a widespread tendency, not an isolated event (see Chapter 7).

Relocating The Problem

Teachers' practical experience, then, points to the broader characteristics of the education system as part of 'the problem.' Once we acknowledge that, a range of issues previously on the margin look more central.

First, we become concerned with the institutional shape of the education system. 'Selectiveness' at its upper levels means a *narrowing offer of learning*, which forces unequal outcomes however much the system favours equal opportunities. If a university system offers places only to 4 in 10 of an age group, 6 must go without degrees.

If unequal outcomes are forced, a struggle for advantage results, and the political and economic resources that can be mobilised in that struggle become important. The poor are precisely those with least assets. In a period when the rich have the upper hand politically, educational policies are likely to be introduced (e.g. mandatory 'objective' testing, 'parental choice' programs) which reinforce the advantages of the privileged and confirm the exclusion of the poor.

Second, we become interested in the economics of education as an issue in social justice. Jonathan Kozol notes differences in per capita spending and the physical state of schools in the U.S. which he calls 'savage inequalities.'[12]

It is, indeed, hard to believe that funding differences of 50 per cent or 100 per cent don't affect educational processes. In Australia there is more equality than in the United States in per capita school funding, but sharper selection for higher education. In both cases, there are major differences in the total *social investment* in the education of rich children and poor children; differences which, on the face of it, massively outweigh *all* compensatory education funds.

Third, we become interested in the school as a workplace or an institution, and how exclusion may be accomplished through its routine practices. 'Ethnographies' of schools can be very helpful in understanding this, even though they make uncomfortable reading. Linley Walker, for instance, shows how conflict and difficulties of control in an Australian working-class high school lead teachers into sexual stereotyping and practices that exclude certain pupils. She speaks of girls not dropping out but being 'exploded' from the school.[13]

Michelle Fine, studying a New York ghetto high school, shows the dull bureaucratic rationality of encouraging dropouts. The 'discharge' of a student becomes the routine solution to almost every kind of problem.[14] Some of my own work shows how state power embodied in the school can become a foil for the construction of masculinity among Australian working-class boys. Once locked into fighting authority via the school, they are, educationally speaking, the walking dead.[15] I hear very similar stories about African-American boys in U.S. schools.

Fourth, we become concerned with the social history of mainstream curriculum and pedagogy, now being mapped in important research by Ivor Goodson and others.[16] Here the very concept of 'mainstream' must be called in question, as it suggests reasoned consensus. What we are dealing with, rather, is a socially dominant or *hegemonic* curriculum.

It derived historically from the educational practices of European upper-class men. Not surprisingly, it embodies their distinctive perspective on the world. This curriculum became dominant in mass education systems during the last 150 years, as the political representatives of the powerful succeeded in marginalising other experiences and other ways of organising knowledge. The current strife in the U.S. over multiculturalism and 'political correctness' (a slogan intended to discredit supporters of multiculturalism) is extremely interesting as a continuation of that struggle.

Finally we become concerned with changes in the social role of education and of organised knowledge as a whole. As I noted before, we are currently involved in a long-term shift in the relation of organised knowledge to the economy. The education system has become not only a strategic gatekeeper to labour markets but also a major force of production, through its role in producing and codifying knowledge.

The explosion of 'credentialism' in the last generation has given education a new weight in the production of economic inequality. The internal division of labour in the education industry itself — from the president of Harvard University to the janitors at Thomas Jefferson High in Brooklyn — becomes a strategic component of inequality in the society as a whole.

A New Geography Of The Problem

With these points in mind, I will try to outline the new geography of the problem that seems to be emerging. This starts, like the old geography, with a 'poverty cycle;' but the concept

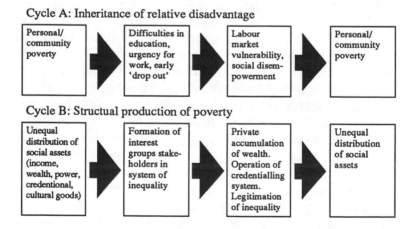

Figure 2.
Poverty cycles. Source: R. W. Connell, K. M. Johnston and V. M. White, *Measuring Up*, Canberra, Australian Curriculum Studies Association, 1992.

needs a little restructuring.

The steering of young people towards different educational and economic fates has to be located within the social processes that create unequal 'fates' to be steered into. There is, we might say, a *second poverty cycle*: the production, shaping, legitimation and reproduction of structures of inequality. It is an 'advantage cycle' as well as a 'poverty cycle.'

Education is not, as older social science pictured it, a mirror of economic or cultural inequalities.[17] That is all too still an image. Education systems are busy institutions. They are vibrantly involved in the *production of social hierarchies*. They select and exclude their own clients; they expand credentialed labour markets; they produce and disseminate particular kinds of knowledge to particular users.

Further, education is centrally involved in the *creation of social identities* for groups who are stake-holders in the system. These identities range from narrow old-school-tie networks, to broad professional ideologies of international scope.

On a wider scale again, education is central to the modern *legitimation* of inequality. Education systems persistently promote the belief that people who are advantaged in the distribution of social assets *deserve* their advantages. They deserve a better deal because they are more intelligent, or better trained, or more hardworking, or because they and their parents have sacrificed to get these assets.

Equal opportunity programs in education, ironically, rest on this belief in merit, and reinforce it. To the extent they do reinforce it, they help to discredit those who continue to be failed.

The model of a 'cycle' is at best an approximation. Ultimately we need to replace it with the idea of *history*. That is to say, we need to understand the way relationships between education and other social institutions are constantly being reconstructed. Compensatory education programs emerged in the later stages of the postwar boom. The widespread belief in continuous economic growth made it possible to get political support for measures to expand 'opportunity.' But within a few years these measures were being undermined by the growth of structural unemployment, the increasing pressure on women as heads of households, and the resulting growth of child poverty in the 1970s and 1980s.

The growing importance of organised knowledge in production and distribution systems has intensified the class struggle for advantage in education and training. This is the key reason why compensatory programs have never been enlarged to the scale where they would have major redistributive effects.

Though the school is a distinct institution, with walls and doors of its own, education is never a closed system. Schools are interwoven with their milieux. Their design and functioning presuppose relationships with families, workplaces, labour markets, and neighbourhoods; and the way schools are designed, as Dorothy Smith notes, presupposes that these other institutions are organised in particular ways.[18] For instance, the length of the school day presupposes that an adult is in the home during normal adult working hours, i.e. it assumes a non-employed mother. The custom of setting 'homework' presupposes a home where schoolwork can easily be done; and so forth.

Looking at it from the other end, from the perspective of neighbourhoods and families, conducting these relationships with schools requires various resources.

Some of these are very familiar, and are the bread-and-butter of conventional research on educational disadvantage: health, nutrition, physical security, emotional security, attention from helpful adults, peer support, time available for schoolwork, books in the home, scholastic know-how in the home, etc.[19] We might call these *contextual resources* for schooling. They represent the material and personal supports of formal schooling, focussed on the individual learner.

Less familiar, often quite absent from conventional research, are the kinds of resources involved when property-owners cap taxes that support public schools — as happened in California with the passage of Proposition 13 in 1978, producing a long decline in that state's school financing. Or when universities dominate curriculum and examination boards. Or when, in the Boston area, the parents of mostly white, affluent Lincoln find parent-teacher relationships running on wheels, while the mostly Black and Hispanic parents of poor Chelsea find them jagged and abrasive.

This capacity to shape a school system to one's needs involves what we might call *collective resources*. Sometimes this involves political mobilisation, but more often it is a question of the routine functioning of institutions.

The inequalities of contextual resources in a given time and place, and the deployment of collective resources by the groups involved, define the historical situation that an education system finds itself in. The central feature of this situation, from the point of view of social justice, is the *situational relevance* of curriculum and pedagogy.

Nine out of ten educational sociologists emphasise the importance of some cultural match between school and home, and nine out of ten sociologists cannot be mistaken! But they may be a little off the beam. Most formulations of this point, including Pierre Bourdieu's well-known conceptions of 'cultural capital' and 'social reproduction,' are too static.[20] Even dominant groups do not seek simple 'reproduction' through education. They know the world is changing, and they want the schools to help their children get ahead of the game. The shift to coeducation in ruling-class schools and elite colleges is a notable case in point.[21]

Chapter Three

Knowledge, Objectivity And Hegemony

Society And Knowledge

There is a very general principle behind the connection of distribution and content discussed in Chapter 1. Knowledge itself is social, it does not exist in some ethereal realm outside society. The organisation of knowledge that we are familiar with in school curricula was created by particular social processes, by particular people with particular points of view.

This becomes obvious when we look at it across cultures. There is a fascinating anthropological literature about growing up and coming of age. I recommend to anyone who is interested in the shape of the curriculum as a whole, the experience of reading a good description of childhood in another culture.[1] It is a quick way of learning how very specific are our own understandings of what is proper or necessary learning.

But not everyone has the time or inclination to read anthropology. And those who do still have to confront the widespread belief that the mainstream curriculum is holy writ. This is a crucial point, where the policy argument for reform often stalls. Practitioners and politicians object: surely knowledge is knowledge, science is science, great literature is great literature — and the school (on behalf of the society) wants all children to acquire them?

To answer this objection requires us to look at where curricular knowledge comes from. The case of natural science is central. As Thomas Kuhn and other historians and sociologists of science have shown, scientific knowledge does not exist as isolated facts, and is not produced by isolated geniuses struck by wandering apples.[2] Scientific knowledge comes in large chunks — paradigms, disciplines, theories, research programs, etc. Scientific knowledge is produced in a highly organised social process. Research communities, research institutions, communications networks, are the social milieux required for scientific knowledge to be produced.

These social milieux are located in social structures, and are necessarily shaped by them. There is a powerful (though complex) link between the rise of modern physical science and the rise of modern capitalism. Some fascinating recent research by Evelyn Keller, Sandra Harding and others has shown there is also a link with gender. Western physical sciences were constructed specifically by men, through activities and forms of speech that reflect men's dominant place in the social and natural world. In areas like medical science this involved a conscious, and largely successful, attack on healing practices and health knowledge associated with women.[3]

Once produced, knowledge still has to be selected or compiled to make a curriculum. This is not done in heaven by a committee of epistemological angels. Historical research has traced the creation of school 'subjects' like geography by inquiries, syllabus committees, academic entrepreneurs, and bureaucrats.[4]

The creation has not been smooth. There have been struggles for space in the schools' offerings, struggles over prestige and dominance for particular bodies of knowledge. Herbert Spencer's 1859 essay 'What Knowledge is of Most Worth?', arguing the case for natural science against classics, is one of the great moments in this struggle. Taken-for-granted ideas about what are 'basic skills,' what are the 'core' areas of knowledge, and how knowledge itself is divided, are all products of an intricate politics shaped by the wider distribution of social power.

Once compiled, curriculum knowledge does not float about

the school as a kind of academic ectoplasm, but is embodied in classroom and whole-school practices. Curriculum is not only a statement of what is to be learnt by the students, it is also a definition of the teacher's work — it describes a labour process.[5] It is therefore unavoidably shaped by the organisational and industrial demands of the school and school system, and by the occupational and professional needs of teachers as a workforce.

A key product of these imperatives is a system of assessment and educational selection. The importance of assessment in controlling and shaping curriculum knowledge is historically shown in the role of matriculation-level examinations, from the Leaving Certificate to the Higher School Certificate, in shaping Australian secondary education as a whole.[6] It is recently shown by the importance that conservatives in the United States, up to and including former President Bush, have attached to the installation of a national standardized testing system as a means of control over schools.

Assessment systems are potent because they shape the *form* of the curriculum as well as its more obvious *content*. An individualized, competitive assessment system shapes learning as the individual appropriation of reproducible items of knowledge and the individual cultivation of skills. (I will go into these issues in more depth in Chapter 6.)

This has important consequences for justice. Such a conception of learning produces, as a cultural effect, a belief in the unequal educational *merit* of individual students. For a wide variety of reasons, pupils' appropriation of knowledges and cultivation of skills proceeds at different paces and along different paths. Competitive assessment produces a particular *interpretation* of this fact, as a sign of unequal merit — or intelligence, learning capacity, talent, diligence, educability, achievement (there are innumerable variants on the idea).

It is important to register that social effects were not just built into the curriculum in the distant past. The same thing is happening now, as curricula are revamped and updated.

Let me give an example from a rapidly developing area, computer education. The social point of view which is most visible in computer education is the point of view of the computer companies. Imagine a school which is *sponsored* by a computer company: where the company supplies the school with a considerable number of free computers, provides software, and sends company staff to the school to advise on how to use the gear. The principal of the school will be touchingly grateful for this, and will say things like, 'We will be trying to incorporate computer technology into every part of the curriculum.' The company will then use the school's name, and photographs of the school's pupils using its products, in its corporate advertising.

Not a Clockwork Orange scenario, as it happens. I am quoting from a lengthy advertisement that appeared in an Australian teacher journal in 1990.[7] It pictures a high school in the public system, 'sponsored' by the Toshiba computer company, which has done all the things I mentioned, including the quoted statement from the school principal.

Now the process of learning among adults involved with computers is not at all like conventional classroom instruction. The process is highly informal, and is based on networks, often on friendship networks. It involves an enormous amount of sharing equipment, knowledge, tricks of the trade, software, and so on. There is a whole category of software which computer buffs distribute to whoever needs it, free of charge: it is called 'shareware.'

Much of *this* kind of learning and teaching is regarded with deep disfavour by the computer companies. Some of it, indeed, is defined as 'pirating,' and the company may prosecute if you let on what you are doing. The computer firms believe in 'intellectual property,' private property in knowledge. This is the logical *opposite* of the ideal of knowledge in a public education system. It is not difficult to guess which perspective on computing is being built into the curriculum at Toshiba High.

A typical consequence of social class divisions in schools is the splitting of the curriculum. 'Academic' work tends to get separated from the kind of learning that occurs in an engineering shop, a bakery or a steno pool. The latter comes to be treated as a subordinated or inferior kind of curriculum, associated with the education of subordinated social classes.

So far I have been emphasising the way social division and social power shape the production and distribution of knowledge. But the social character of knowledge has two sides. The recipro-

33

cal is also true: the way knowledge is organized has social consequences. The curriculum produces social *effects*, not incidentally but through its very nature as an organization of knowledge.

If a curriculum is organised as the individual appropriation of bits of hierarchically-organised abstract knowledge, measured by competitive individual assessment, then that curriculum will reliably produce class division. In *Making the Difference* we called this the 'hegemonic curriculum' in Western school systems not only because it holds a dominant position within the schools, but also because it helps to generate and reinforce class hierarchy in the society as a whole.

This curriculum has a more complex relationship with gender division. Though it was historically produced out of the educational traditions of boys' schools, it also became a vehicle for the advancement of certain groups of girls. Sara Delamont's intriguing study of elite women's education in Britain shows that this chance could only be grasped by super-conformity to social conventions of femininity — hence the otherwise ridiculously rigid dress codes and emphasis on decorum that have marked middle and upper class girls' schools.[8]

Working-class girls were not invited into this charmed world: they were not obliged to wear gloves on the tram. But as mass secondary education developed, it became possible for *a minority* of working-class girls to contemplate pushing their way up, via success at the hegemonic curriculum and entry to semi-professional jobs. This even became an agenda for some feminist teachers in public schools. Here the hierarchical character of the hegemonic curriculum has become the basis for a splitting of forms of femininity in working-class schools. Much the same is true of forms of masculinity: selection and streaming, academic success and failure, are important bases for the production of a protest masculinity all too evident in the 'discipline problems' of working-class schools.[9]

These observations hardly exhaust the topic of the relations between knowledge and its social context, one of the most complex problems in the social sciences. But they are perhaps enough to establish that we need to reckon with the question of how knowledge is produced and organized. If we are to pursue justice in the schools, then we need a standpoint on curriculum design that gives priority to these issues.

Common Learnings And Objective Knowledge

Any curriculum must make a selection from possible knowledges and possible methods; and there is no general guarantee of the correctness of that selection. For this reason, some sociologists have seen the basis of curriculum as an *arbitrary* cultural content.[10] But no selection of knowledge or method is neutral with respect to the structure of the society in which it occurs. In that sense the notion of a 'cultural arbitrary' is a fiction — and a potentially damaging one. For it implies that epistemological relativism is good enough as a critique of mainstream curricula. But simply endorsing a pluralism of alternatives is not a sustainable strategy.

A curriculum necessarily intersects with the relationships of inequality in society that constitute social interests. This is not merely the point that there are social bases for particular curricula, as we have seen. A curriculum, as an ongoing organization and distribution of knowledge, helps to *form* social interests, and arbitrate between them. A common learnings program, i.e. a curriculum which seeks to include the whole school population, embodies relations of hegemony among interests and groups in the society it deals with.

Definitions of common learnings cannot arise from abstract definitions of human need, as if child development took place in a social vacuum. They exist, rather, as *programs* for the organization and transmission of knowledge, programs which attempt to bring the educational process into a particular relationship with social forces. Such programs arise in definite historical circumstances, are promoted by particular interests (or alliances of interests), have specific social effects, and have greater or less worldly success.

For example, a particular organization of knowledge and method, which was first called 'natural history,' then 'natural science,' and increasingly just 'science,' was institutionalized in schools and universities in the 19th and early 20th centuries. As historical research now shows, this form of knowledge and method embodies a quite specific set of gender relations. It expressed a dominant form of masculinity, and its power over both femininity and the natural world.[11]

This masculinity was not pre-formed. In fact, the rise of natural science and industrial technology was part of the historical process by which new forms of masculinity were constructed. A rationalized and calculative masculinity, at this time, was displacing forms of masculinity organized around traditional patriarchal authority, honour, and personal violence, as the leading form in ruling-class life. The stock market was replacing the duel as the test of dominance.[12]

By the mid twentieth century the sciences constructed along these lines had become the leading component of the academic curriculum. They displaced Latin and literature, in a process that will be familiar to teachers more than 45 years old. The social consequences of this process included the cultural exclusion of women from the newly dominant forms of knowledge, and from careers based on them — the exclusion that 'equal opportunity' programs in science and technology are now grappling with.

The definition of common learnings that is institutionalized in the academic curriculum, its language, and its practices of learning and assessment, also results in a general exclusion of working-class students from the world of higher learning and the resources to which it gives access. The process is complex and subtle, but the effects are powerful. They include not only the statistical exclusion of working-class youth from higher education, but also the cultural intimidation of the labour movement. In many parts of labour politics we have reached the point where the leadership is unable to conceive of any form of working-class educational advancement except getting more of the hegemonic curriculum.

To acknowledge these facts of history is not to be committed to a belief in relativism, where any 'alternative' is as good as any other. The intellectual strength of the hegemonic curriculum is its claim to embody objective knowledge. That claim cannot be effectively contested by denying the idea of 'objectivity,' as many radical critiques do. These critiques are right in pointing out that curriculum as an organization of knowledge always has particular social bases, and advances particular social interests. But that argument shows that knowledge is inherently *socially constructed*, not that it is inherently subjective, or non-objective.

'Objective' does not mean abstracted or divorced from a situation — as positivist ideology would have us believe. On the contrary, in the social sciences at least, highly abstracted knowledge is likely to be exceptionally distorted and misleading — the opposite of objective.

A recent example is provided by the controversy in Australia over the cutting of funds for migrant education, such as English as a Second Language (ESL) programs. These cuts were justified by studies that purported to show, objectively, that there is no migrant disadvantage in education. The studies were highly abstracted, generalized surveys, typically done by people with little or no grass-roots experience of ethnic education. They had no awareness of where in practical experience the problems were known to be; hence they lumped together, in the one statistical category of 'migrants,' groups which had severe language and acculturation problems with groups which did not.[13]

People have great trouble breaking out of the conventional dichotomy that contrasts 'objective' with 'subjective,' and 'neutrality' with 'bias.' It is nevertheless essential to do so, to realise that knowledge can be socially constructed *and* objective. The philosopher Max Deutscher has pointed the way through this difficulty.[14] Knowledge, he points out, always has a context, since the knower lives in the social world. Being objective, gaining accurate and undistorted knowledge, requires a subjective *commitment* within that context, an *engagement* with the issues.

Subjectivity and objectivity, then, are not opposites. Objectivity is a characteristic of the process of discovery (or of learning) which is fuelled by subjectivity.

Objectivity, we might say, is methodological; subjectivity is relational. Objectivity can equally be a characteristic of quite different relationships to the social world. (If that sounds paradoxical, think of spy novels. In Le Carré's famous series both the British and Russian spymasters, Smiley and Karla, show a high degree of objectivity in reasoning and enquiry — though their purposes are diametrically opposed! If you haven't read *Tinker Tailor Soldier Spy*, think of Sherlock Holmes and the arch-criminal Moriarty in Conan Doyle's story.)

Given this basic point about knowledge, it becomes possible to think of common learnings programs which are quite as *objective* as the currently hegemonic curriculum, but which are constructed from other social standpoints, and give priority to other social interests.

The mainstream curriculum is hegemonic in schools in the sense that (a) it marginalizes other ways of organizing knowledge, (b) it is integrated with the structure of power in educational institutions, and (c) it occupies the high cultural ground, defining most people's common-sense views of what learning ought to be. As I showed in *Teachers' Work*, this curriculum's position in the schools is bolstered by its close connection with teachers' professionalism and self-confidence — though it is also undermined to the extent that it comes to be recognized as a source of teachers' occupational problems in mass schooling.

The mainstream curriculum is hegemonic in the society at large in the sense that it is part of the cultural and practical underpinning of the ascendancy of particular social groups — capitalists and professionals, men, Anglos.

To move beyond relativism, the idea of many equally-valid 'knowledges,' without buying into the particular definition of knowledge contained in this hegemonic curriculum that condemns excluded groups to continuing exclusion, is to embark on a strategy of *inverting hegemony*.

This strategy accepts the need for a program of common learnings in the schools, but does not accept the basis on which common learnings are currently constructed. The strategy seeks a way of organizing content and method which builds on the experience of the disadvantaged, but generalizes that to the whole system, rather than confining it to an enclave. The strategy thus seeks a practical reconstruction of education which will yield relative advantage to the groups currently disadvantaged. It attempts to turn a defensive, compensatory strategy into a pro-active, universalizing strategy.

In principle there are many possible common learnings programs, though in practice only a few are likely to be of importance in a given time and place. A minimal criterion for choosing between them is provided by the first principle of curricular justice described in the next chapter, the interest of the least advantaged.

I say this is 'minimal' because there are epistemological as well as ethical reasons for seeking an educational program constructed in this way. Common learnings programs are not born equal. Different social standpoints yield different views of the world, and some are more comprehensive, more epistemically powerful, than others.

This is a classic proposition in the sociology of knowledge, and a major reason why a sociological view of knowledge need not collapse into relativism in the way notions of the 'cultural arbitrary' do.[15] If you wish to teach about ethnicity and race relations, for instance, a more comprehensive and deeper understanding is possible if you construct your curriculum from the point of view of the *subordinated* ethnic groups than if you work from the point of view of the dominant one. 'Racism' is a qualitatively *better* organizing concept than 'natural inferiority' — though each concept has its roots in a particular experience, and embodies a social interest.

In general the position of those who carry the burdens of social inequality is a better starting-point for understanding the totality of the social world than is the position of those who enjoy its advantages.

This is a structural argument about bodies of objective knowledge, not an argument about the quantities of information held by individuals within a particular hegemonic organization of knowledge. As is well known, on tests and examinations constructed within the paradigm of the hegemonic curriculum, working-class children on average do worse, i.e. they appear to have *less* knowledge. (For all the effort that once went into devising a 'culture-free' intelligence test, no such thing has ever got into circulation. For good sociological reason: neither intelligence nor information is a culture-free thing.)

What are the reasons for thinking the standpoint of the least advantaged is a better starting-point for curriculum making? At its simplest, this standpoint yields experiences and information not normally available to the dominant groups, and therefore overlooked or marginalized in their constructions of knowledge.

A familiar example is the traditional school history curriculum centering on the deeds of famous men, now vastly expanded by the deeds of un-famous men, and the deeds of women. The history thus produced is certainly better in being more comprehensive, truer to life 'as it really happened.'

But simply being more comprehensive is only the beginning. When Georg Lukacs, one of the founders of the sociology of knowledge, discussed the 'point of view of the proletariat,' he had in mind a point about intellectual power.[16] The structural location of the working class at the point of production revealed to workers, in the most concrete way possible, the basic mechanism of capitalist accumulation through the extraction of surplus-value from labour. However sophisticated other points of view might be, because they did not have this as a guiding insight they could not grasp the dynamics of capitalist society.

In a classic demonstration of the importance of standpoint in constructing knowledge, Lukacs went on to explore with great subtlety the blockages in European philosophy that resulted from the philosophers' location in the world of capitalist privilege. In Lukacs' argument the standpoint of the proletariat would be crucial in overcoming these blockages, not because factory workers are better analysts than philosophers, but because the insights arising from their experience and action are necessary to allow the reconfiguration of the whole domain of culture that alone can solve the philosophical dilemmas.

What Lukacs argued for the case of class relations applies with surprising precision to the case of gender relations. There have long been bodies of information about the family, women's employment, sexuality, children's social development, masculinity and femininity. They remained for decades a backwater in social sciences hegemonized by the interests of men. So far as such topics appeared in social theory at all, they did so via concepts like 'sex role' and 'modernization.'

The standpoint of the least advantaged in gender relations, now articulated in feminism, has transformed these fields. Modern feminism has produced a *qualitatively better* analysis of this large domain of social life.[17]

Partly this was done by bringing to the fore experiences that had been little discussed before — such as sex discrimination, sexual harassment, or the experience of mothering. Perhaps more importantly, it was also done by developing new concepts and a new kind of social theory — embodied in terms like 'sexual politics,' 'patriarchy,' 'sexual division of labour' and 'gender relations.' These concepts allowed a major reconfiguration of the existing domain of knowledge, as well as the addition of experiences not previously included. The conceptual revolution resulting from this is still going on in the social sciences, and its effects are still to be felt across much of the school curriculum.

With both class and gender, an understanding of the central mechanisms producing a social structure is available through the experience of the groups *subordinated* by those mechanisms, not through the experience of the groups advantaged by them. To try to explain this would require a general theory of ideology, which is a little beyond the scope of this book; all I hope to do here is register the importance of the point for curriculum.

To say this understanding is 'accessible' through a group's experience is not to say it is necessarily produced in fact. Producing it, and then generalizing it, requires constructive intellectual work. And this is not easy for disadvantaged groups to do, precisely because of their disadvantage: most of the tools of intellectual work are in other people's hands. The complex issues that arise at this point are very lively ones for teachers in disadvantaged schools.

The task is complex and difficult, but possible. If the necessary intellectual work is done, the point of view of the least advantaged becomes the basis of a program for the organization and transmission of knowledge, which provides a common learnings agenda for all schools.

It is then possible, in principle, to construct a comprehensive educational program, a common learnings program, whose claim to preference over the existing academic curriculum is twofold. First, it follows the principle of social justice in education by embodying the interests of the least advantaged. Second, it is intellectually better than other ways of organizing knowledge.

This gives a clearer meaning to the strategy of inverting hegemony. It is not just a matter of changing the beneficiaries (as in the old Polish joke: Capitalism is the exploitation of man by man; and Communism, comrade, is the reverse). It is also a matter of overcoming the blocks that current power structures offer to our shared intellectual and cultural advance.

In such a framework, counter-sexist curriculum, working-class curriculum and multi-cultural curriculum cease to be names for curriculum enclaves or oppositional standpoints. They become principles for system-wide democratization, and collective intellectual growth.

No one who is familiar with contemporary schools will make the mistake of thinking this reconstruction will happen next week. Powerful social interests oppose it; the hegemonic curriculum has been widely challenged but its hegemony remains. Nevertheless we have many starting-points for change, and in the second part of this book I will explore some of the practical issues that arise in pursuing these principles.

Chapter Four

Curricular Justice

Three Principles Of Curricular Justice

On what principles can we operate in trying to grasp hold of these processes and turn them in the direction of social justice? What are our design principles, so to speak, for a curriculum that will lead towards social justice?

I suggest three principles, taken together, might constitute a workable model of curricular justice.

(1) *The interests of the least advantaged.* One of the key concepts in the philosophers' discussions of the nature of justice is caring for the worst-off first. John Rawls proposes that education must specifically serve the interests of the 'least favoured' groups in society. The principle of advantaging the least advantaged is central in Rawls' general theory, and captures what is usually meant in public politics by talk of 'social justice,' even in the limited sense of social justice policy statements.

The 'standpoint of the least advantaged' means, concretely, that we think through economic issues from the standpoint of the poor, not of the rich. We think through gender arrangements from the standpoint of women. We think through race relations and land questions from the standpoint of indigeneous people. We think through questions of sexuality from the standpoint of gay people. And so on.

(I would argue that this is not only a matter of social justice. It is also likely to be a source of enormous enrichment for the experience and knowledge of the advantaged groups, in all the cases that I have mentioned. But this is not to say that taking this standpoint is easy for advantaged groups. Justice is not a question of ease and it is the opposite of anaesthesia. At the best of times it is likely to mean trouble. But as Michael Walzer argues, such a conception of justice is a practical one, it is about justice 'here and now.'[1])

This principle has strong implications for curriculum, which become clear when we think about the social history of curriculum and the way the current hegemonic curriculum embodies the interests of the *most* advantaged. Justice requires a *counter*-hegemonic curriculum, in the sense outlined in Chapter 3, designed to embody the interests and perspectives of the least advantaged.

What this means in practice is being worked out by teachers in a variety of settings: compensatory education programs, multicultural education, programs for girls, indigeneous people's education, certain adult literacy programs. In Chapter 7 I will discuss one of these experiences in detail; here I will make two general points about this and other cases.

First, social justice is not satisfied by curriculum ghettos. Separate-and-different curricula have some attractions, but leave the currently hegemonic curriculum in place. Social justice requires moving out from the starting-point to *reconstruct the mainstream* to embody the interests of the least advantaged.

Second, social justice is not satisfied with one counter-hegemonic project. Contemporary social science recognises, as contemporary social practice does, a number of major patterns of inequality: gender, class, race, ethnicity, and (on a world scale) region and nationality. Curricular justice requires counter-hegemonic projects across this whole spectrum. In practice there will be great diversity in what is undertaken. I am not trying to lay down a blueprint here, but to indicate the scope of the principle of curricular justice. No institutionalized pattern of social inequality is in principle exempt from it.

To recognise that knowledge can be organised differently,

and that different ways of constructing it will advantage and disadvantage different groups, is to risk falling into relativism. There have been education systems where the political outcome is the key criterion for curriculum choice. This was the case in the Soviet Union, and the far right in the U.S. is doing its best to impose the same logic in that country.

It is important to avoid this, as it would abandon the element of independent truth in, for instance, scientific accounts of the world; and therefore the possibility of *critique* of the political agenda itself. (To notice that these accounts are shaped by gender and class is not to say that gender and class are their only content; they also document an encounter of a gender- and class-shaped consciousness with the natural world.)

The principle of the interests of the least advantaged provides a clear motive for avoiding relativism, since it cannot be in their interest to continue being excluded from that knowledge of the natural world that is embodied in conventional science. A counter-hegemonic curriculum must include the generalisable part of the conventional curriculum, guaranteeing all students critical access to scientific methods and findings.

(2) *Participation and common schooling.* School systems commonly claim, in statements of goals, to be preparing future citizens for participation in a democracy. Thus the Australian Education Council, the ministers of education in Australian state and federal governments, included in their recent declaration of ten National Goals for Schooling in Australia:

> To develop knowledge, skills, attitudes and values which will enable students to participate as active and informed citizens in our democratic Australian society within an international context.[2]

If we take this purpose seriously — and I am not for a moment suggesting that ministers of education usually do — it has major implications for curriculum. The notion of 'democracy' implies collective decision-making on major issues in which all citizens have, in principle, an equal voice. Major issues in modern states include war and peace, investment, employment policy, urban development and environmental protection, sexual violence, social welfare provision, the content of mass communication, and the design of education systems.

To be active participants in such decision-making requires a range of knowledge and skills (including the skill of getting more knowledge). This range is required for *all* citizens, as Walzer forcefully argues. You cannot have a democracy in which some 'citizens' only *receive* decisions made by others. That is why feminists are right in pointing out that a society in which men routinely exert control over women is no democracy.[3]

Here is the basis of a common curriculum which must be provided to all students *as a matter of social justice*. This is a much stronger criterion than the invocations of 'democracy' in the National Goals imply. This criterion rules out all selection, competitive assessment, streaming and classifying mechanisms in schooling while the common curriculum is in operation, since such mechanisms differentiate offerings and therefore advantage some citizens over others.

It points, rather, to ungraded and cooperative learning practices in respect of the common curriculum. They should be cooperative, since all participating citizens are advantaged (as citizens of a democracy) by each others' learning. In this respect, justice would be significantly advanced by banning all grading and competitive testing during the compulsory years of schooling.

Since a necessary part of the knowledge and skills of participants in democracy is an understanding of the cultures and interests of the other participants, this criterion also rules out curricula produced from a single socially-dominant standpoint. It points firmly towards the principle of the 'inclusive curriculum' proposed by Jean Blackburn and others in the 1980s.[4] This means curricula which include and validate the experiences of women as well as men, Aboriginal people as well as whites, workers as well as professionals.

The attempt to produce a 'diverse' or multicultural curriculum in the United States, currently resisted by conservatives with rhetoric against 'political correctness,' is clearly supported by this principle.

(3) *The historical production of equality.* There is a tension between the criterion of participant citizenship, requiring common curriculum, and the principle of pursuing the interests of specific groups, the least advantaged.

This could logically be resolved by using one of Rawls' devices and introducing a 'lexical ordering' of the principles of curricular justice. Thus we might say that participation has priority, and the criterion of the least advantaged applies *after* the participation criterion is satisfied.

But this would rapidly lead to educational absurdity. It would assume the curriculum can be partitioned into 'participant citizenship' and 'counter-hegemonic' bits. In the realities of teachers' daily work in schools, such a distinction would be impossible to sustain.

If a counter-hegemonic criterion is to be practically useful it must apply to the same educational processes that the participant citizenship criterion applies to, and we must find a way to think these criteria *together.* The tension between them can be handled productively by taking note of the historical character of the social structures producing inequality. Their existence is not that of objects like rocks or planets, but is *a process of producing and reproducing* social relationships.

This means that 'equality' cannot be static; it is always being *produced* in greater or lesser degrees. The social effects of curriculum must be thought of as the historical production of more (or, as the case may be, less) equality over time.

Participant citizenship and counter-hegemonic criteria can then be seen as elements in the same historical process. Dealing with the tension between them is a matter of making strategic judgments about how to advance equality. The criterion of curricular justice is the tendency of an educational strategy to produce more equality in the whole set of social relations to which the educational system is linked.

It is difficult to give a capsule example of such a complex set of relationships, but the general idea can be illustrated by Australian educational intervention in South-East Asian countries. In recent years this has come to be seen as an export industry based on fee-paying students. The 'export' of Australian education to South-East Asia in such terms reproduces over time the privileges of the urban elites in those countries, who can afford to buy professional education for their children. It promotes development, but not democratic control of development.

As Chris Duke points out, its social consequences are quite different from those of aid which works at the village level through informal adult education and institution-building. This kind of education functions to raise the villagers' capacity to articulate their own needs and pursue them over time. One is not surprised to find the elite model is more acceptable to the governments of affluent Western countries.[5]

Unjust Curricula

Principles of curricular justice should help us do some educational house-cleaning — identifying aspects of curricula that are socially unjust and that we might care to get rid of.

(1) The principle of the interests of the least advantaged is negated by any curriculum practice which confirms or justifies their disadvantage. There have been many forms of curriculum for slavery, with the message of the 1848 hymn:

> The rich man in his castle,
> The poor man at his gate,
> God made them, high or lowly,
> And order'd their estate.

Histories of education are full of tragi-comic quotes of this kind, consigning girls to domestic science, workers' children to training in deference and useful labour, Aboriginal children to godliness, cleanliness and illiteracy.

Nowadays no education authority in its right mind would admit to 'ordering their estate,' not intentionally. But they do it all the same. When teachers in NSW public schools objected in 1990 to the Basic Skills Test on the grounds that it mandates failure for the majority, they were making this point. So were the teachers in disadvantaged schools who criticised competitive testing in general because of its dire effects on children in poverty.[6]

So are teachers who criticize streaming because of its effects on the children streamed down:

Here at this school, my very first day with the children having the tests, and then next day putting them into groups, and seeing the children sitting around. And straight away they knew which was the best group, which was the worst group. And hearing a little girl say that she hadn't been picked for any group yet: 'Oh, I hope I get in this group,' and 'Oh, that must be the good group because such-and-such is in it.' And then the last group called out, and she was in it. The dejected way, on the second day of the school year, that she went to that class, knowing that it was the dummy class — that was dreadful. And for all the good things that go with streaming, I would never advocate it, because of that.[7]

(2) The principle of citizenship is negated when the curriculum includes practices that allow some groups to gain a greater share in social decision-making than others.

This may be direct or indirect. Directly, formal education gives social advantages through credentialism, where educational certification is linked to closed labour markets. Curricular practices that give particular social groups superior access to credentials (e.g. academic streaming, which is known to be class- and race-linked) are to that extent unjust.

Indirectly, education may give background legitimacy to the authority or power of advantaged social groups. Privileged classes are legitimated where their representatives are given particular authority in curriculum decision-making — e.g. elite private schools having representatives on boards and committees that determine system-wide curriculum guidelines, where disadvantaged schools have no such representatives. The privileged position of men in gender relations is legitimated (among many other ways) by physical education curricula which highlight competitive sports; given that the main competitive sports are showcases of a dominating masculinity and have the effect of 'naturalising' the superiority of men over women.[8]

(3) The principle of the historical production of equality is negated when change in that direction is blocked. The recent expansion of selective schooling under a right-wing government in New South Wales, a macro-streaming of the secondary curriculum, is an obvious case. The government's intention

seems clearly to have been to produce more inequality.

Less obvious, but more common in educational history, is the blocking of change by the codification of culture. Curricular practices involve injustice when they reduce people's capacity to remake their world. The death of a sense of possibility may be as effective as any positive propaganda for slavery.

All curricula involve codification, of course. But some rest on closed bodies of knowledge and define teaching as authoritative instruction in fixed content. Others embrace cultural change and explore the creation of new meaning. Music teaching provides a striking illustration, with its tension between a closed codification (the authoritative curriculum of the conservatories) and an open one (usually based on rock performance).

Literature is the most visible case, because of public controversy about the literary 'canon.' Here an authoritative codification — the canon of literary classics — has come under increasing criticism for excluding the voices of the less powerful. Alternatives range from trying to develop multiple canons —women's writing, black writing, new literatures in English — to arguments against the very idea of canons and classics.[9]

Curriculum Logics

Our research on the Disadvantaged Schools Program gathered a mass of information about what is actually done by teachers, administrators and parents who are trying to meet criteria of justice in curriculum decisions. Reflecting on this evidence, I would suggest that there are three curriculum logics in actual use, each of which could be generalised into a social justice policy.

(1) *The logic of compensation.* This was central to the initial design of compensatory education programs in the 1960s and 1970s, and is still the commonest way of thinking about questions of justice in education.

By 'compensatory' logic I mean the principle being followed when extra resources are added to the schools serving communities of disadvantaged people. The idea is to bring the disadvantaged to the same table at which the advantaged are already eating.

A concrete example is where school systems go out and buy more computers for schools serving disadvantaged communities. This is a resource issue, of course, but also affects the curriculum. We have data from one Australian state suggesting that the use of computers as a teaching aid in disadvantaged schools is slightly more common than it is in other schools in that system.

(2) *The logic of oppositional curriculum.* This is the approach that flatly rejects the mainstream curriculum. Its supporters say that you don't try to bring the poor to the same table as the rich because that table itself is not level, and the poor cannot get a fair feed at it. The mainstream must be rejected because it is producing the unequal outcomes.

Instead, the principle is to separate out an area of educational practice in which a separate curriculum can be developed, over which the disadvantaged have control. Then they can get the kind of education that fits their needs specifically.

In a limited sense, that logic could be found in technical schools in earlier periods of educational history. There was a system of technical schools, mainly serving working-class communities, staffed by teachers with working-class backgrounds, and tied in to apprenticeship schemes influenced or even controlled by unions. At its best, this could produce an educational ethos which built on working-class experience and ideas about learning.

This was always severely limited, however. It was focussed on boys, and substantially excluded girls; 'domestic science' schools were doubly marginalized. Technical education was always subordinated to academic education in the school system as a whole.

A more vigorous 'oppositional' logic was created, in the early part of the century, in the form of Labour Colleges. They were educational institutions set up, not by the state, but by the trade union movement. They tried to develop a curriculum which grew out of the collective experience of working class people as embodied in the unions. They faded out after a generation or so, but the story is worth recalling. It suggests the kind of educational creativity to be found in working-class organisations which are not normally thought of as an educational resource.[10]

More recently, oppositional curriculum logic is represented in areas like Black Studies, Women's Studies and Aboriginal Studies in the universities and colleges. Again, a part of the curriculum is separated out. Named courses deliberately set out to embody the point of view of the named group in the design of the curriculum. This is not meant to be a top-down, 'we'll study them' kind of exercise, but a collectively produced body of knowledge by a group reflecting on their own experience and history.

The debates about Women's Studies programs in the last two decades highlight the problems of setting up a curriculum enclave. On the one hand, this risks abandoning the rest of the curriculum to the social forces that the movement was setting out to challenge. It lets academics off the hook, in terms of the content of other courses: 'We don't need to put women into History 101, that's taken care of in Women's Studies...' On the other hand, it creates a serious status-and-resources problem for the enclave, which is likely to be defined as very low on the academic status ladder and therefore starved of resources — a common experience in fact for Women's Studies programs. That sets up pressure to make Women's Studies more academically respectable, more theoretical or more technical — which also has happened in practice. And that moves it away from the political purpose for which it was set up in the first place.[11]

(3) *Counter-hegemonic curriculum logic.* (My apologies for the jargon.) This approach attempts to *generalise* the point of view of the disadvantaged rather than separate it off. There is an attempt to generalise an egalitarian notion of the good society across the mainstream. That remains the basis for curriculum thinking as reform moves out from the standpoint of the disadvantaged to reconstruct the system as a whole.

Let me give an illustration from the history of computing. The Apple and Apple II were the first widely popular small computers. It is not widely known that the design of these machines had a political motive.

A group of progressive people in the American computer industry, influenced by the radical movements of the 1960s and 1970s, were critical of the domination of information technology by mainframe computers, by big business users, and by the enormous monopoly company IBM. They argued that information technology ought to be democratised, and set about trying to design a kind of computing that would be widely accessible. In the late 1970s and early 1980s they achieved spectacular, if qualified, success.[12]

Counter-hegemonic strategies are known, though not often named, in school systems, both at the policy making level and at the level of school practice. An interesting example comes from the work of the Australian Schools Commission in 1985. Among the goals proposed for the Disadvantaged Schools Program (then administered by the Schools Commission) was the idea of ensuring

> that students have systematic access to programs which will equip them with economic and political understanding so that they can act individually or together to improve their circumstances.[13]

That got watered down in translation into the actual program guidelines; but at least in its initial formulation, the goal was a counter-hegemonic one in the sense I mean here.

An example from higher education is the sociology curriculum at Macquarie University, where I worked for a good many years. We attempted to design substantial parts of it on counter-hegemonic principles. For instance, in designing our courses on gender we tried to create a program of study which covered areas of sociology traditionally organized around other concepts (e.g. 'the family,' 'deviance'), reorganizing the curriculum in ways that gave priority to the perspectives of women and gay men. This included new material, of course, but it did not move off the terrain of the traditional discipline; rather it claimed that knowledge and attempted to reorganize it.

An example from practice in schools is the "Hands On" computer learning package produced by a group of disadvan-

Figure 3.
Counter-hegemonic curriculum, a concrete example. Source: *Hands On, The Computing Kit*, Sydney, Cluster Productions, 1988.

taged schools and a regional service centre in Sydney (see Figure 3). This involves an approach to computer learning which emphasises not only the techniques of handling your Toshiba but also the social implications of computers in the workplace.

The package was produced in a disadvantaged setting, and used the experiences of disadvantaged kids and adults with the new technology. But it is capable of being used across the whole system — of being exported, so to speak, beyond the context of disadvantage. And this has indeed been done.

Finally, as an example of the wider development of these ideas, I will mention the 'Essential Curriculum' project. This has grown out of a secondary school DSP network in Sydney. It has attempted to generate a structure for curriculum as a whole, in a way that embodies the principles of social justice spelt out above. It has been produced by teachers and grows out of experience in particular schools, but has the potential to be applied to a whole school system.[14]

These are three curriculum logics that can be developed from the starting point of social justice. They do not necessarily exclude each other. I suspect that an effective social justice program in schools would move through all of them in some way or another. There is, nevertheless, a logical development from the first to the third, in terms of scope and long-range potential.

PART TWO:
PRACTICALITIES

Chapter Five

Work For Teachers

Teachers And Change

In thinking about any serious educational reform, in the cause of social justice or for any other purpose, it is essential to consider what it means for teachers.

This is not because teachers are an inherently suspicious or conservative bunch, naturally opposed to change, who have to be Got Around somehow. That is a view of teachers now being promoted by neo-conservatives; it helps to discredit teachers' unions, and to promote managerial control of the school system. Ideas like 'teacher-proof' curricula (which I find an extraordinarily offensive idea: try 'parent-proof' childrearing, or 'executive-proof' businesses) go together with an economic interest in keeping public schooling costs down.

Rather, it is because teachers are central to what happens in education. Educational reforms eventually have to work through teachers, and worthwhile educational reforms have to work with them. It is simple realism to recognize that teachers make or break most educational reforms, depending on how they take them up.

But it is not just Machiavellianism for anyone proposing education reforms to think about teachers' responses to them. Teachers have a right to be considered, and consulted. They have an important stake in the education system, and any democratic process of educational change must involve them as active participants.

Teachers also have perfectly legitimate industrial interests. Like any other group of workers they have rights to reasonable conditions, satisfying work, control over their own labour, reasonable pay. It is not reasonable for other players in educational affairs to expect teachers to pay the cost of reforms by loss of such rights.

Beyond the question of rights, teachers can be a vital resource for change. They, more than any other group of adults concerned with schools, know where the shoe pinches — where things are not working well. Teachers have, among them, an enormous fund of experience and ideas which *if tapped* represents a tremendous asset for progressive reform. (I emphasise 'if tapped,' as a remarkable number of education policy proposals do *not* seek to draw in teachers in a substantial way.)

Finally, teachers can be the strongest of forces making for educational change. There are, of course, cases where teachers have opposed change; but there are also many cases where they have been the key advocates. Most teachers like the kids they work with, and want to do their best for them. When teachers become persuaded that certain changes are in the interests of the kids, and do not react negatively on their own conditions of work, a powerful force for change is created.

What *are* the interests of teachers, and how do they bear on questions of social justice in education? To answer this question we have to look at the nature of teaching as work, the school as a workplace, and teachers as a workforce.

Work And Workplace

In the last decade and a half a good deal of research and thinking has been done on these topics, which allows us to think more clearly about the social role of teachers.[1]

In the first place, there has been attention to the nature of teaching as a kind of work. Like other groups of workers, teachers are engaged in a labour process, that fills their working day with a series of tasks and links them to other workers in the same workplace.

Teachers' labour process is unusual, however, in having an 'object' that is very difficult to specify. The object of labour for other workers might be a piece of steel, or a pile of insurance forms; but in teaching it is something like the minds of the pupils, or their capacity to learn. It is no wonder that even experienced and highly skilled teachers make remarks like this:

> I don't know enough about what I'm doing. I don't really know how to teach, except by the feel; because I don't really know how people learn. I don't think anybody does. I think what we're doing is very hit-and-miss.[2]

It is no wonder, either, that the definition of the teacher's task can expand and contract in alarming ways. The popular image of schoolteaching is talk-and-chalk in front of a class, and this is indeed a central part of the teacher's craft. But even talking at a blackboard implies other tasks — preparing the lesson, preparing materials, settling the class, keeping order, supervising exercises and correcting them. Beyond that, teachers do an extraordinary range of things in and around schools. I once tried to list all the jobs done by teachers I could find mentioned in a set of interviews, and gave up after I had reached nearly eighty and was still going strong.

It is understandable, then, that questions of total workload are important political issues for teachers. More subtly, questions of the weight given to different components in the mixture are important, such as the ratio of time spent with kids vs time spent on paperwork, or time spent in keeping discipline vs time spent helping kids to learn. Where a school is not functioning well as an institution, the time and energy spent on simply keeping order may rocket up, and this is one of the frustrations often referred to by teachers in disadvantaged schools.

In most schools that I know of, the tasks — however defined — are addressed with a set of craft skills that make the difference between an effective teacher and someone just treading water. I say 'craft' skills because they are impossible to convey in formal training programs, as we are reminded by teachers' vivid, sometimes lurid, memories of their First Year Out. These skills include ways of conveying information, ways of managing groups, ways of relating to pupils, ways of managing time, and ways of managing one's own emotions.

Experienced teachers may develop these craft skills to a very high level, becoming locally recognized experts at, say, mathematics for Year 11, or dealing with troublesome junior high classes. Some teachers, having survived the baptism of fire in the first few years, stick with tried and true methods for the rest of their careers. Others consciously innovate, seeking out new techniques, new equipment, or new specializations.

The practical importance of these craft techniques in schools makes the impact on teachers' skills a significant question about proposed reforms. Michael Apple and his co-workers have pointed to the ways in which commercially packaged curricula marketed to schools in the United States (along with packaged tests) tend to de-skill the teacher, or to replace familiar teachers' skills with new ones (such as the clerical skills involved in using the new tests).[3]

It is not clear how far such de-skilling has gone in the teaching trade as a whole. But it is clear that a potential for de-skilling is widespread, in reform proposals that locate control over the teacher's labour process in school management or commercial enterprises.

In disadvantaged schools, there are specific de-skilling possibilities in the little cults that arise from time to time around charismatic characters or nifty ideas, which become popular with press or politicians as ways to turn around 'failing' schools: Strong Leadership, or Learning Contracts, or Direct Instruction, etc. It is interesting that there has never been a cult of Empowered Teachers; perhaps we should try to start one.

The curriculum normally does not figure much in discussions of teachers, and certainly not in discussions of teacher unions and teachers' collective action. This is deeply ironic. The curriculum, as well as being a definition of the pupils' learning, is also a definition of the teachers' work. Different curricula create different tasks for teachers, and imply different patterns of control over their labour. Teachers as workers have a great deal at stake in discussions of curriculum.

The hegemonic curriculum in current use, the competitive academic curriculum (CAC) discussed in Chapter 3, is closely linked to teachers' professionalism. Teachers, after all, are folk who have done well at this curriculum; it is important in their claim to knowledge, in their selection and training. The hierarchy of institutions that is so conspicuous a feature of the Western educational scene (elementary schools, secondary schools, colleges, elite universities), is closely bound up with the hierarchical design of the competitive academic curriculum.

Yet CAC is also an important source of teachers' difficulties — especially though not exclusively at secondary level. The sifting and sorting of pupils that is an important feature of CAC, based on the process of individual competition in tests, defines large groups of *losers* in the competition. These pupils may be sorted out into lower streams, or non-academic 'tracks' or 'sets,' or concentrated in particular schools, or they may just hang around bored at the back of classrooms, but *they are always there* — CAC guarantees it. And teachers have to deal with the consequences.

Many teachers, in trying to do this, become engaged with other curricula that do not follow the logic of CAC. Such curricula already exist in schools, indeed some of them are very familiar. An example is the mastery-learning, non-competitive, practice-oriented education that occurs in art classes, physical education classes, music classes, cookery, metalwork or other craft classes. These subjects can all be reconstructed as CAC, which does happen when they become credentialized (sport becomes the academic subject 'human kinetics,' painting is replaced by art history, etc.). But for the most part they follow a different logic from CAC, and have a subordinated or marginalized place in the school's offerings.

This offers a different way of seeing teacher professionalism. Rather than professionalism being bound up with CAC, it can be defined in terms of the *difficulty of the teaching task*. Work in disadvantaged schools, in this perspective, would be regarded as the pinnacle of professionalism, not as an unpleasant duty to be got through on the way to more rewarding fields of endeavour.

This is, of course, the way many experienced teachers in

disadvantaged schools do see the matter; but there is not much institutional support for their point of view. Among other things, current teacher training programs (with certain honourable exceptions) pay remarkably little attention to issues about teaching in disadvantaged schools.

Not only do we need to think carefully about the implications of teaching as work, we also need to think about the character of the school as a workplace.

As in other workplaces there is a system of authority and control. Obvious features are the school administrative apparatus (principal, heads of department, etc.) and financial arrangements (links to the school board, department of education, etc.). Less obvious features are the legal framework of public education and the informal balance of power among the personalities and factions among a school's staff.

Workplace control of course extends into the classroom and out to the yard as well; teachers are not only subject to controls but are expected to exert control over the pupils. Indeed, the quickest way to get known as an incompetent teacher is not by failing to convey knowledge, but by 'losing control' of one's classroom.

There is, we might say, a *political order* in the school as an institution, a set of arrangements and divisions that define who has authority or power, and over what. This political order is not fixed, but shifts as personnel change, new issues arise, mobilizations occur. In the last two decades, for instance, very large numbers of schools have had their political order contested by the mobilization of women teachers, no longer willing to accept the authority of men but demanding their share of resources and promotions, and demanding attention to the specific interests of the girls they teach.

The political order within a school is an important determinant of the way it will deal with educational reforms. Hierarchical school regimes are not likely to look kindly on curriculum reforms that emphasise participation and student decision-making. But the issue gets complicated, because energetic principals may use a position of authority to promote democratic ideas among staff and parents; decentralized structures may enter gridlock with conflict between departments; and so on.

In general, however, I think that the more democratic the political order of a school, the more likely it is to deal effectively with issues of social justice. Democratic structures are more open to initiatives from below, and a flow of innovations is very important to disadvantaged schools. Democratic structures are also more open to debate, and however frustrating those endless meetings may get, debate gives the chance for subordinated and marginalized interests to find a voice. It is no accident that the Disadvantaged Schools Program in Australia, seeking to maximize community participation in disadvantaged schools, also became a centre of workplace democracy (see Chapter 7).

Being a teacher is not just a matter of having a body of knowledge and a capacity to control a classroom. That could be done by a computer with a cattle-prod. Just as important, being a teacher means being able to establish human relations with the people being taught. Learning is a full-blooded, human social process, and so is teaching. Teaching involves emotions as much as it involves pure reasoning.

The emotional dimension of teaching has not been much researched, but in my view it is extremely important.[4] Teachers establish relations with students through their emotions, through sympathy, interest, surprise, boredom, sense of humour, sometimes anger or annoyance. School teaching, indeed, is one of the most emotionally demanding jobs I know of. The university teaching I do is demanding enough, and that involves a great deal less face-to-face contact than school teaching.

I am not suggesting that teaching should be less emotionally demanding — this is not an aberration, it is a condition of educational relationships in schools. But I would argue that the issue needs to be taken account of more systematically in educational reform. Teachers in schools often experience reform proposals as another moral pressure, as an extra demand on top of the load they are currently carrying.

Good teachers in disadvantaged schools regularly perform astonishing (and unheralded) feats of human relations, overcoming age, class and ethnic barriers, breaking through resentments, suspicions and fears, to establish workable educational relationships. An effective social justice policy for schools will see this as a crucially important educational process, and will work to support it rather than making it harder.

'Supporting it' means providing resources (especially time), teacher autonomy (because human relationships cannot be planned), advice (especially from networks of other teachers), and recognition (that this is an important part of teaching). 'Making it harder' is much easier to do. All you need is to insist on pupil Time On Task, tell teachers they are slack and need to get Back to Basics, demand increased teacher productivity, throw in a few standardized tests, and presto! the job is done.

Recognizing schools as workplaces and teachers as workers has further implications for social justice strategy, when teachers are considered as a group. Teachers collectively form a workforce, and the character of that workforce bears on issues of social justice. We need to consider, for instance, how socially representative the teaching workforce is; how it is selected and trained; what are its paths of promotion and pattern of unionization.

In relation to disadvantaged schools, is the workforce different from the workforce in schools as a whole? And should it be? We need to think pro-actively about the kind of workforce that would be best, in terms of social justice policy, and how (through training, recruitment, promotion or other practices) we might get such a workforce.

I can offer some starting-points for thinking about these questions, as our study of the DSP in Australia included a survey which allows a comparison of teachers in disadvantaged schools with teachers in the rest of the system.[5]

Teachers In Disadvantaged Schools

The Disadvantaged Schools Program is a national compensatory education program designed in the early 1970s. Its original planners relied on teachers for ideas as well as implementation. In this they were responding to a ferment already going on among teachers, including groups debating the social dimensions of schooling. One such was the radical Inner City Education Alliance in Sydney. An activist recalls the moment:

It was 1973 when the Alliance began and I came into it after a couple of meetings. They were already writing the philosophical outline and for the first time people seemed to be talking about the particular problems in the inner city with working class and ethnic kids. It still wasn't acceptable to be talking about 'poverty' in educational circles but this group started saying that the social context was very important for teaching. And we all began reading and discussing and it was a really exciting period.

Activist networks of this kind were important in giving shape to the program in the 1970s, especially in formulating demands for new curricula and for participatory decision making. Yet groups with articulated social radicalism have always been a minority in the teaching force.

The reality of compensatory programs is that they are embedded in an institutional system. Most of the activity in disadvantaged schools is funded by conventional recurrent funds, and managed through the usual routines of the school system. A typical DSP grant might provide a language specialist for a year, in a school with 15 full-time permanent teachers funded by the system. (Generally, a primary school with 300 or so children would receive between $10,000 and $25,000 each year, and a secondary school with 500 students up to $40,000.) This situation is typical of compensatory education programs in other countries, which generally top up system funding but do not replace it.

The extent to which the program is embedded in a larger school system became very clear in our 1989 survey of public school teachers in the state of Victoria. This study obtained a random sample (duly stratified by primary/secondary level, metropolitan/non-metropolitan location, and school size) of teachers in DSP and in non-DSP schools. We thus have a way of finding out how distinctive teachers in disadvantaged schools are, in one of the larger systems, across a considerable range of characteristics and practices. A selection of the findings is shown in Table 1.

There is a difference in average age. Teachers in DSP schools, being younger, tend to have higher initial qualifications. Yet the difference is not large in absolute terms — two years on

			DSP	Non-DSP	Probability
Age	Mean		36.2	38.4	<.001
	S.D.		8.1	8.9	
in-service	Mean		4.5	4.2	n.s.
programs attended	S.D.		4.6	5.3	
in last 3 years					
Father's	Managerial/professional	%	40	42	
occupation	Routine white-collar	%	59	58	n.s.
	or manual				
Union	Active member	%	30	25	
membership	Member	%	66	73	
	Non-member	%	4	2	n.s.
Sense of influence	Mean		3.4	3.5	n.s.
on curriculum	S.D.		0.9	1.0	
issues (scale)					
Rate 'academic	'Very important'	%	42	53	
progress' as goal	Less than 'very	%	58	47	<.005
of teaching:	important'				
Rate 'securing	'Very important'	%	32	33	
suitable job' as	Less than 'very	%	68	67	n.s.
goal of teaching:	important'.				
Use TV, video	'Frequently'	%	21	23	
as teaching aid	Less often	%	79	76	n.s.
Use text books	'Frequently'	%	15	31	<.00001
as teaching aid	Less often	%	85	70	

Table 1

Comparisons between DSP and Non-DSP teachers in Victorian government primary schools, 1989.

average. There is little difference in current training, as illustrated in Table 1 by the item on in-service programs attended.

No substantial differences in social background appear. Contrary to some folklore in the program, disadvantaged schools do not tend to attract teachers from disadvantaged backgrounds. Organisational activity, including unionism, runs at the same level in schools inside and outside the program.

Looking inside the school, practice seems very similar. Teachers in both DSP and non-DSP schools report the same low sense of influence on administrative decision making, the same slightly greater sense of influence on curriculum issues. Resources available are broadly similar, apart from the consultants and aides specifically funded by the DSP.

Outlook on teaching, and use made of facilities, are likewise fairly similar. The main exceptions are the tendency of teachers in non-DSP schools to place greater stress on academic goals and formal curriculum sources such as textbooks, while teachers in DSP schools place more stress on negotiation.

These results point to the determining power of the system as a whole. Where teachers in DSP schools collectively do show a difference it is a shift of emphasis, often little more than a nuance within the overall pattern.

This finding is particularly impressive given that DSP schools are, by definition on an Index of Disadvantage, extreme cases. They do pose extreme problems, and the teachers register this. One of the strongest differences to appear in the study is on two questions asking for comparisons with the teacher's previous school. More than twice as many teachers in DSP schools as in non-DSP schools describe their present school as 'more difficult,' both in discipline and in helping students to learn.

Despite this, the practices followed in DSP schools are, overall, not very different from those in the rest of the system. 'Pin money,' as one activist called the compensatory funding, cannot fund an educational revolution. To put it another way, system or professional routines remain powerful even in situations of exceptional need.

This general point made, the survey provides evidence of adaptation in details. These include a de-emphasis of conventional academic goals; less reliance on formal teaching methods and sources such as textbooks; and greater reliance on negotiation and participation. This pattern becomes clearer when we look at teachers who have relatively long service in DSP schools. On most points where teachers in DSP schools differ from system norms, experienced DSP teachers differ from less experienced DSP teachers; they are DSP — only more so.

Here is evidence, if not of an educational revolution, then at least of a 'DSP ethos' borne by the more experienced teachers.

Evidence from the oral histories and the interviews with program administrators extends this side of the picture. One of the central facts about the program is that over time it has built up a core workforce, including experienced classroom teachers and also specialist teachers, consultants (parents as well as professionals), committee members and administrators.

This 'core' is organised very informally, it is a network rather than a cadre. But its presence is critical. It gives a degree of continuity to a program which could be — given the submission basis of funding — extremely fragmented.

The network provides an informed audience for policy debates, such as those about 'quality proposals,' 'per capita funding,' and other issues. It is the main bearer of the accumulated practical knowledge about what does and does not work in disadvantaged schools. And at times, particularly given its overlap with parent organisations and teacher unions, it has provided vital political support for the program.

There is a cycle here which is difficult to disentangle. In pointing out how an activist network has contributed to the program, we must also register how the program has taught the activists. One of the least obvious but perhaps most important functions of the program has been its role as a teacher educator.

In some schools new teachers are deliberately introduced to the ethos of the DSP and the issues it is confronting. A principal describes the process:

> One thing I have done is where I've had a parent take all our new teachers on trips around the neighbourhood. I give them two weeks to get an idea of what the places look like. She takes them out for half a day to various parts of the neighbourhood and then goes to another parent's home where they talk about what it's like living in the area. We get a parent who has had some contact with the school, but not someone who's president of the parent club or on the School Council. Some teachers find it a bit frightening, some have said it is really good. A lot of our teachers are from the country. They finish their four year country service and when they come down here they are in a state of shock. But I want to get to them early before they settle into bad habits.

Among the first generation of activists the bonding and debate could be so intense that it took over a teacher's life. Another principal recalls:

> We developed a staff that was very committed, very hard working and close knit. A large number of them came because they wanted to work with me because I'd worked with them before,

or because they know that the school stood for new open plan teaching and working class kids. They were young, enthusiastic. And the school was very demanding on them, more than I think in retrospect that it had a right to be. I guess my administrative style added to that. I expected a hell of a lot of commitment. It placed huge demands on the people and on their personal lives. If I can exaggerate for a bit, relationships within the school were so strong that any outside the community didn't really have much chance of survival. So marriages broke up — and I wouldn't do that again. And my own kids will tell you that I changed over that period. I gradually disappeared out of their lives more and more. And I think that is typical of the DSP.

We end up, then, with a split image of the program's work-force. On the one hand is evidence of intense commitment by a network of people who have poured emotional commitment and long hours of unpaid labour into making the program work. On the other hand is the evidence of a teaching work-force not radically different from that of the system as a whole.

Both pictures are true. Taken together, they give a sense of the incremental way educational reform works.

Finally, in understanding this process, we should not ignore the impact of the DSP on the larger system. Through the normal career progression of teachers in a school system, program experience gets spread around. One of the most interesting findings of the survey is that in the sample of teachers in non-DSP schools some 29 per cent reported having at least one year's experience in DSP schools, and 19 per cent have 3 or more years' DSP experience. If the program is working as a teacher educator, some at least of its influence should be spread around the rest of the school system. It seems likely that this would also be the case for compensatory education programs in other countries.

Teachers As Reformers:
The Political Field In Education

It is a cliche that teachers are, or ought to be, non-political. Teachers are expected to keep out of party conflicts, at least in their job as teachers. Teachers are expected not to use their classrooms for propaganda; or, more exactly, they are expected to propagandize only for the established order, with pledges to the flag, 'O Canada' in chorus, and pictures of the president or Queen.

The character of teachers' work and teachers' workplaces, as outlined earlier in this chapter, makes nonsense of the idea that teachers can be non-political. Politics concerns the distribution of resources, conflict between interests, the uses of power; and all of these things happen in schools and through schools, unavoidably. As Terri Seddon puts it:

Teachers' work, which involves conscious and unconscious processes and effects, is both shaped within, and in turn shapes, relations of power. Teachers' practice in economic and cultural production creates asymmetries in individuals' and groups' capacities to define and realise their needs. Teachers' work is therefore also political action because, consciously or unconsciously, it serves to confirm or contest the prevailing social order.[6]

This is so in general terms, as a result of the nature of teachers' work. But what does it mean in specific terms, for a democratic educational agenda concerned with social justice? How can the politics become conscious?

We can usefully think of a democratic agenda as operating at two levels: democratising the workplace, and democratising the work.

Democratising the workplace means, at the most basic level, expanding the power of base-level workers in schools. Whether this is called 'industrial democracy' or just 'participation,' it involves expanding workers' control over their own labour process, and workers' involvement in controlling the collective life of the workplace.

Since workplaces in the public sector, like those in the private sector, are usually managed on quite different assumptions — assumptions of managerial prerogative, 'leadership,' or more straightforwardly, dictatorship — democratisation is rarely accomplished without struggle. In such struggle, the organized industrial power of workers is critical. That is to say, democratisation of the school as a workplace very much depends on the vigour of unions among teachers and other workers in schools.

The drift of recent reforms in education systems, in Australia at least, has been in another direction. Attempts to dismantle the centralized bureaucracies that used to govern school systems have been accompanied by the growth of fiscal controls over schools, and the conversion of the school principal from the senior teacher in the school into a kind of bureaucratic entrepreneur. The new managerialism, now rampant in other parts of the public sector besides education,[7] has particularly serious consequences for a social justice agenda.

Democratization *in* the school is not necessarily the same as democratization *of* the school, for there are other people involved as well as those who have jobs in the school. Relations with the surrounding community are particularly important, and particularly difficult, for disadvantaged schools. Parents are likely to have had worse than average experiences with schooling in their childhood; while community poverty means that the resources available for dealing with educational issues are low.

For both these reasons, community participation via conventional channels in disadvantaged schools is likely to be slight. Finding ways of balancing community participation with industrial democracy, or better still making them work together, is an important part of a social justice strategy.

Democratising the work, in current educational contexts, means above all transforming the competitive academic curriculum. This is the site of the main social exclusions that occur through education, and the rationale for most of the hierarchy within educational institutions.

While the fact that this curriculum is hegemonic testifies to the power of the social interests that support it, there are many resources for contesting and displacing it. Other curricula are present in the schools and offer models of other ways to teach and learn, even if they are currently marginalized. Some powerful cultural forces, most of all the popular concern with children's welfare and the child-centred interest in development and expression, give support to more humane and child-centred pedagogies. The political forces pushing for more testing, tighter discipline, and more basic Basics, certainly do not have it all their own way.

In the contests that surround CAC, a key role is played by the issue of assessment. Neo-conservatives often speak of making teachers more 'accountable,' and the usual accountability mechanism they have in mind is standardized testing of the pupils. Defence of the academic content of CAC often involves reference (though the arguments begin to get circular) to the assessment processes of selection for higher education. People urging social justice agendas have, on the whole, been slow to address assessment issues, and it is important to do this. Accordingly, in the next chapter I will look at the different models of school assessment in terms of their implications for social justice.

Democratising the work also means opening teaching/learning processes up to groups who have been excluded from them, or from control over them. This goal has been formulated in some recent discussions as the goal of an inclusive curriculum, as discussed in Chapter 4. Multicultural education, specific educational programs for girls and for indigenous children, and incorporation of working-class experience, are examples of what is meant.

We need to think about the implications of these movements for teachers' labour process. To some extent, these innovations have been included in school systems' offerings by intensifying the division of labour, notably by designating particular teachers as specialists in particular groups of pupils. While this is an obvious way of getting started, it is dangerous if this is where the process ends. This would lose the richness that the new material in principle brings to the old curriculum. Multiple curricula, rather than multicultural or multisourced curricula, would result.

But if 'diversity,' as it is currently called in the United States, is to become a guiding principle for the curriculum as a whole, there are significant implications for teachers as workers. For one thing, the training most teachers have had is seriously inadequate on this front. For another, routines of classwork and assessment that presume a single 'culture' need to be rethought and reworked; and this demands time and resources. It seems to me that diversity in the curriculum will, in the long run, set up pressures towards more systematic team teaching, more systematic in-service training (on a regular basis rather than the chancy and episodic basis that is usual now), and more inter-school networking.

In all of this, the starting-point is clarity about who teachers are and what they do. There is so much myth and rhetoric hanging about education that simple clarity is not easy to come by. It matters that teachers are employees, most of them public servants; that sets up a specific relationship with government. It matters that they are moderately privileged, but not wealthy, employees; that sets up a specific relationship with families and children in poverty. It matters that they work under major constraints of time (which are not easily visible to people outside the trade) and under the pressure of prevailing assessment and certification systems. All of these forces can be grappled with, and to some extent overcome; they cannot be ignored.

Chapter Six

Assessment

In this chapter I want to explore the ways assessment systems bear on the issue of social justice. There is a lot of confusion of terms about 'measurement,' 'assessment' and 'evaluation.'[1] I will use the term 'assessment' to mean the appraisal of pupils and their learning, however that is done — via tests, examinations, teacher's records, self-appraisal, or whatever. By 'evaluation' I mean the appraisal of programs or institutions.

The starting-point for the analysis has to be the social character of education systems, and the production of inequality within them. Education systems, as I have been arguing, are large and powerful social institutions. They are internally hierarchical, and as I have argued in Chapters 1 and 2, they are deeply involved in the production of social inequalities; they do not merely reflect them. With the growth in the economic importance of organized knowledge, and the growth of credentialism in labour markets, this effect of education systems has doubtless been growing in importance in the last two generations.

The analysis in earlier chapters shows that social inequalities are generated in a number of educational processes: the determination of curriculum, selection and streaming, the creation and award of credentials, and the legitimation of hierarchy by creating ideologies of educational merit. Educational *assessment* is, evidently, deeply involved in the process.

Yet the production of inequality in education is an inherently contradictory process: not least because of its clash with the criteria of justice also at work in school systems. We can expect this to be a politically turbulent area, with contradictory demands being placed on schools. There will constantly be openings for moves towards more equality as well as moves towards more hierarchy.

The questions that arise about assessment of children in poverty are urgent, but they are not unique. They concern the most severe effects of wider inequalities. Because they are the most severe, these effects warrant special attention, and special programs. But they will be completely misunderstood if they are thought of as *exceptional*. Strategies to deal with them only make sense in the context of broader social justice thinking, and policies of wider scope. For that reason, we must start with the assessment system that is hegemonic in the school system as a whole.

The Hegemonic System: Standardized Competitive Assessment

Schools serving children in poverty are parts of larger education systems. This institutional context is the main determinant of the way they work. Our survey of disadvantaged schools in Victoria found that in most respects their practices were very little different from schools elsewhere in the same system. And why should we expect otherwise? — given that the system provides, in more or less standard form, the architecture of the school, capital works, recurrent funding, teacher training, administrative routines, promotion structures, zoning systems, and the legislative framework of public education.

Part of this systemic context is a system of assessment. In Western school systems, and Western-style school systems elsewhere in the world, a particular assessment regime is hegemonic. This means both that it is culturally dominant, connected with the society's central structures of power; and that it functions to maintain the social power and prestige of dominant groups.

This does not mean that it is the *only* assessment system in the schools. There certainly are others, just as there are non-hegemonic curricula in schools. But they are subordinated or marginalized, in quite concrete ways.

The hegemonic assessment regime is, of course, intimately connected with the hegemonic curriculum already discussed. In this curriculum, learning is defined as the individual appropriation of pieces of knowledge and skills. The content to be appropriated is defined authoritatively in advance. In contemporary education systems, the ultimate 'authority' for curriculum content is provided by academic disciplines in the universities. Academic disciplines in provincial universities are in their turn given authority by the metropolitan universities. It is not conspiratorial, but merely realistic, to say that the dominant curriculum in Canadian or Australian schools is in the final analysis guaranteed by the prestige of Harvard, Oxford and the Sorbonne.

This knowledge is, in principle, abstract and generalizable, not tied to particular learners or social settings. The knowledges and skills are arranged hierarchically. Access to them is regulated by a formal sequence of learning, often involving selection of the learners. (Thus, certain content is in principle only taught to medical students, who have qualified for medical school by a string of prior performances; etc.)

The dominance of the competitive academic curriculum (CAC) is nowhere written in fire as divine law. It was historically produced by the social struggles which shaped modern education systems. Nevertheless its hegemony is now very firmly established. Among other things it has been built into teacher selection and teacher training, so it is close to the heart of many teachers' sense of professionalism. This is an important fact about the preparation of teachers for work in disadvantaged schools — or the lack of preparation.

The competitive academic curriculum requires a suitable assessment system. This will measure the individual appropriation of the pieces of knowledge and skills defined in CAC. Judgments by the assessors (since all assessment is ultimately a social judgment of one person by another, however mediated by machines) place each individual learner in a hierarchy against a background of other individual learners. This is done tacitly in traditional examinations; and explicitly in modern standardized tests.

The assessment procedures, like the contents of CAC, are

abstracted from particular contexts. They claim to be neutrally generalisable, and their claim to fairness rests (uneasily) on this claim. A sequence of tests of increasing difficulty, through a pupil's career, matches the hierarchical organization of CAC content.

Like CAC, this assessment system has gone through a historical evolution. The rote learning test and the literary examination were followed by the IQ test, and that in turn by the standardized attainment test. All are still in use in classrooms. The current assessment scene is an archeologist's delight.

Nevertheless the last half-century has seen increasing importance given to the standardized or normed paper-and-pencil particulate (short-answer with additive scoring) test of capacity or attainment. This has been the central assessment device used in the *evaluation* of educational programs using the familiar Tyler model of evaluation.[2] It has also come to be a major assessment device in making decisions about individual pupils, developing attainment 'profiles,' etc.

Schools or systems whose assessment regimes centre on such tests may be said to have a Standardized Competitive Assessment (SCA) regime. A modernized equivalent of the old examination system, it is now the typical accompaniment to the competitive academic curriculum.

These assessment practices, installed for purposes of surveillance, selection and credentialling, have been integral to the educational exclusion of the poor. I do not think there is any great mystery about this. The positive correlation of 'test results' with 'socio-economic status' that is so familiar a result in educational research should only surprise those who think testing is a socially neutral, purely technical, activity. On the contrary: testing is a form of social judgment, and the correlation with social class is, in a basic sense, *intended*.

That this result will be produced is guaranteed not only by the *content* of the testing, which generally presupposes vocabulary, information, etc. more likely to be found in middle- or upper-class homes than in working-class or rural homes. It also has to do with the *form* of testing. SCA testing is marked by abstraction from context, reliance on paper-and-pencil skills, absolute individualism, and a competitive framing of the activity. All this resembles the occupational, family and cultural world of the administrator, the professional, and the businessman much more closely than it resembles the world of the factory hand, the road maker, the supermarket cashier or the agricultural labourer.

SCA weeds out the poor and legitimates the advantages of the privileged. Yet it would be wrong to say it is 'biassed,' in the sense of being arbitrarily unfair. There is nothing arbitrary about it. SCA results generally feel right to teachers and pupils alike, in a conventional classroom situation. More often than not they match teachers' gut feelings about 'talented children' vs 'dull children' or 'slow learners.'

Against accusations of bias, SCA claims objectivity. I am sure this claim is, in an important sense, correct. For instance, SCA does, impersonally, identify some 'bright' working-class children and promote them through the education system.

The point is, this objectivity is the mode of functioning of an unequal social and educational order. The interplay between an unequal society, and a hierarchical and selective education system, yields inequities which SCA impersonally and objectively reflects back. The more objective such an assessment system is, the more effectively it legitimates the inequalities generated by the system as a whole.

Getting Beyond Competition:
Descriptive Assessment And Alternative Credentials

The effects of SCA and similar assessment regimes are highly visible in schools serving children in poverty. They mean chronic failure, disaffection from schooling, and self-blame. These effects are present in the memories of working-class *parents* as well as in current experiences of children. Though some parents have warm memories of their own schooling, many recall boredom, violence, meaningless learning tasks, and a desire to get out as soon as they could.[3] Teachers in disadvantaged schools can be eloquent — and bitter — about the way SCA systems corrupt or block their educational work.

This experience has provoked a search for alternatives, and there has been a certain ferment on assessment issues in and around disadvantaged schools, an attempt at renovating the system from below.

The changes that result are often no more than minor adjustments to make the hegemonic system more humane — amendments to the motion, rather than rival principles. But two substantial alternatives have emerged from this ferment in Australia, and they have parallels in other countries. They centre on the notions of 'descriptive assessment' and 'alternative credentials.' I will call the resulting assessment strategy the DAAC approach, for short.

School renovation centering on descriptive assessment is best presented by example. The Appendix gives, in brief, two cases from our study of assessment and evaluation in the Disadvantaged Schools Program. Martin Street School is an elementary school which undertook a schoolwide renovation of assessment under its own steam, choosing one of its own staff to become the assessment 'expert' — a kind of barefoot-doctor approach. The renovation centred on developing a 'pupil profile' folder which was a cumulative collection of samples of work and teacher observations.

Wells High School is a secondary school where assessment reform was originally undertaken in one department, and then spread from that base. This reform also centred on cumulative descriptive records, but in this case more closely tied to specific learning objectives.

These are examples of the main direction taken by school-based reforms in Australian disadvantaged schools, a push towards non-competitive individual descriptive assessment.

Movement in this direction has not been as rapid as many teachers would have liked. It is hampered, above all, by the way the secondary curriculum is tied to selection and credentialling at the end of high school. This is widely recognised, and has led to attempts to change the credentialling process. Debate has centred on the idea of alternative credentials.

This became possible with the diversification of the secondary curriculum in the last two decades, which followed the growth of comprehensive high schools. It became a major issue in Australian education at the end of the 1970s, when the numbers staying on beyond year 10 rose, largely because of higher levels of youth unemployment. Schools were confronted with a new late-adolescent clientele with little interest in the competitive academic curriculum.

The usual response was to offer alternative programs which diversified the curriculum, and allowed more control of assessment to classroom teachers. In New South Wales a considerable range of new subjects were inserted in the existing Higher School Certificate, under the rubric of 'Other Approved Studies.' In Victoria, alternative curricula were grouped under separately named credentials and a separate division within the HSC. The 'separateness' and 'other'-ness of these arrangements is an important issue, which I will come back to.

Credentials issued under SCA usually report assessments in the form of summary numbers — marks, deciles, 'bands,' letter grades etc. This form of reporting drastically abstracts from the context and the material character of the performance being reported — as is required by the logic of SCA.

Attempts to remedy this abstraction have led to the *descriptive credential*, combining descriptive assessment and alternative credential. A well-developed example is the Record of Achievement designed by the Inner London Education Authority (shortly before that Authority was abolished by the Thatcher government). This credential consists of a dossier, the content being negotiated between pupil and teachers, that presents a cumulative sampling and appraisal of the pupil's work.[4]

Attempts to introduce DAAC have run into other problems besides mayhem-bent governments. An obvious and important one is teachers' workloads. The micro-technology (as we might call the set of tools, skills and rules at the base of an assessment system) involved in descriptive assessment readily leads to information overload and too much work for teachers.

The purpose of descriptive assessment is, after all, to widen the focus of observation to include a greater range of the students' behaviour. More of the child's life is exposed for recording and filing in the folder: moral as well as cognitive capacities, states of mind as well as quality of work. 'Some people went overboard collecting examples and doing all sorts of complicated and intricate charts,' remarked one Australian teacher about this.[5] The information so painstakingly collected was often not put to use, the files mouldered. Who, in the pressured atmosphere of a disadvantaged school, has the leisure to read, let alone reflect on and interpret, bulky folders of previous years' work and observations?

There is also a civil-liberties issue about descriptive assessment. The more continuous and wide-ranging the assessment, the more intensive is the surveillance of the child. Pupil records may contain material on emotional states and refer to family conflicts. These records are used in 'case consultations' between teachers and social workers. They *may* even be called for in court proceedings; they are not legally privileged, and I have heard of one case where this happened. Given the existing surveillance of poor families by the state, and attempts at control of their behaviour (now intensifying as governments attempt 'behaviour modification' on the poor via the welfare system), this is not a minor issue.

Having DAAC as an alternative in assessment and certification does not in itself overcome the effects of SCA. Generally the alternatives do no more than *fragment* the assessment process, either by radically individualizing it, or by creating a second stream of assessment and credentialling. This exists alongside the mainstream, and is marginalized by it. The terminology of 'other approved studies' and 'alternative assessment' shows well enough which foot wears the boot.

The danger is that without a direct challenge to SCA, the alternative system will basically institutionalize the disadvantage of the groups it was set up to serve. The alternative credential is regarded as a second-rate credential, and special deals have to be negotiated to allow pupils access to universities.

In one important Australian case, an attempt has been made to resolve this problem too. In Victoria under the recent Labor government, ideas from the 'alternative' streams were built into a *single* secondary credential intended to replace both the former SCA mainstream credential, and the former alternatives to it.

The Victorian Certificate of Education (VCE) is a notable innovation which deserves to be widely known. Its introduction involved a vast and complex negotiation between administrators, teachers, universities, employers, parent groups, etc. There is no doubt that its principles were watered down before its introduction in 1991. This did not save it from furious attacks by SCA diehards, which played into conservative political agendas; and the VCE in its present form will probably not survive the new-right government elected in 1992. Nevertheless the experience is important. It shows that a social justice strategy, which gives priority to the educational interests of the disadvantaged, is feasible in credentialling too.

A limit the VCE does not transgress is the focussing of assessment on the individual learner. Indeed, descriptive assessment regimes may go further towards individualism than SCA. This is especially likely in elementary schools, where descriptive assessment is often praised because of its ability to reflect what is unique about each child. This is an appealing theme to teachers of a humanistic, child-centred outlook; and makes sense to parents, who are often (wrongly) assumed to be rigidly attached to old-fashioned 'marks.'

But extreme individualization of assessment sits uneasily with the needs of working-class and disadvantaged children. For economic deprivation is a social fact and a shared experience, not a trait of an individual. It needs collective action to remedy; and we must therefore consider what assessment practices might be relevant to that collective practice.

Getting Beyond Individualism: Equity-Based Assessment

The DAAC approach has opened certain spaces in the school system. In these spaces teachers, pupils and parents can, on local initiative, set up assessment systems that are less damaging to working-class interests than the mainstream one is. Given the significance of assessment as a means of control over curricular knowledge, this is a valuable help in sustaining forms of knowledge, and ways of learning, in which working-class interests are advanced — and with them, the interests of children in poverty.

Yet this gain, as I have just argued, is limited. Is it possible to go further?

To move beyond the position reached with DAAC requires

an approach to assessment that is *positively equity-based*. By this I mean an approach which introduces questions of equity or social justice to the *foundation* of our thinking about curriculum and assessment. Typically these issues are raised at the end of the discussion, when we look at a distribution of outcomes from some assessment process which up to then has been treated as a question of technique.

An Equity-Based Assessment (EBA) approach would start from the fact that teaching and learning is inherently a social process, a complex process of inter-action, any aspect of which can raise questions of social justice. Assessment practices are never technical devices that are socially neutral. They are, in their essence, social techniques. They have, inevitably, social consequences.

This is true even when it is concealed by the assessment regime itself. It is characteristic of the micro-technology involved in SCA that it takes the social relations of learning, and foreshortens them into aspects of individuals, calling them 'attainments.' One of the most powerful effects of SCA is to persuade the public that the outcomes of learning can only be understood in this individualized way. DAAC follows suit, for the most part.

This is precisely where an equity-based assessment approach diverges. EBA must concern itself with the appraisal of the social process of learning *as a social process*.

Though this is an unconventional view in the assessment trade, it is not a new idea. A charming piece in this vein was once written by the Canadian academic and humourist Stephen Leacock.[6] He suggested, in an essay on the Oxford University system, that its success was due to the frequency with which tutors smoked pipes while hearing their students' papers — "Men who have been systematically smoked at for four years turn into ripe scholars" —and to the university's fine indifference to the "measuring of 'results' and... this passion for visible and provable 'efficiency.'" Oxford, in short, relied on close social relations between teachers and taught, not on SCA.

The question at the centre of EBA is not 'where does the pupil stand?' but 'how well is this teaching/learning process working for the pupils?' — *all* the pupils.

Since answering assessment questions is a social process, and subject to considerations of social justice, a key question is which groups participate in the appraisal, and on what terms: pupils, teachers, parents, neighbours, unions, employers, administrators, or others. With an EBA approach, the predominance of experts in SCA is systematically challenged. Knowledge is required, but authority is not; democratic control over the assessment process is central to the concern for equity.

The micro-technologies involved in EBA may include descriptive assessment. They *may* even include standardized competitive tests, for certain purposes such as establishing resource needs (though I am not convinced about that, given the arguments above about how such tests work). But EBA must go beyond those micro-technologies, for two reasons.

First, equity-based assessment must concern itself with educational outcomes that are *inherently collective*, that cannot be represented or measured as an attribute of an individual.

An important case is 'participation.' Effective participation in public life as a citizen commonly figures as an item among 'objectives of schooling.' Participation in the life of the school is commonly pursued as the educational means toward it. While there are individual differences in levels of participation, at the most basic level participation is the collective achievement of a *group*. No individual, however willing, can sustain pupil participation in school decision-making unless the student body as a whole sustains it — via councils, class representatives, discussion of issues, course planning, or other means. Students, in turn, can rarely sustain a participatory culture unless the school staff also support it — providing the organizational means for representation, providing personal support, good examples, etc. When we assess 'student participation' as an outcome, then, we are inevitably assessing mainly what a collectivity has done.

I would argue that the same is true of the *cognitive* performances at the heart of SCA, which are also sustained collectively. This fact is suppressed by the way the disciplines of educational measurement and educational psychology usually go about their work, so to many people this seems an absurd claim. But a close examination of the conditions of cognitive development, even in accounts like Piaget's which are usually taken to emphasise an unfolding within the individual, will show how crucial is the social process calling out and sustaining cognitive performance.[7]

The second reason why EBA must involve new micro-technologies is that the approach must concern itself with relationships that are much wider than the focus allowed by DAAC or SCA — that apply, for instance, across whole national education systems. However good the teaching-and-learning process looks at Ragged Edge Public School, and separately at Whispering Glades Private Academy, it is *not* going well if the process at the two sites differs in ways that advantage the Whispering Glades community.

This may suggest that what EBA amounts to is replacing 'assessment' with 'evaluation.' Within the current education system this would not be a bad thing to do, if only because it would encourage people to ask larger questions.

Nevertheless EBA is 'assessment' within the definition given at the start of this chapter, the appraisal of pupils and their learning. It is a matter of appraisal based in the day-to-day interactions of the classroom, the curriculum as realized, the actions of particular children and particular teachers.

The difference is that the EBA approach rejects the idea that those events can be understood as if the classroom were sealed in a bottle. This approach sees classroom events as interconnected with wider sets of relationships, which constitute classroom life as well as being constituted by it. The approach concerns itself with pupils as social beings, not monads; and with 'pupils,' i.e. the subjects of learning, as collectivities and populations, not only individuals.

These remarks about EBA are fairly abstract, though the concerns and experiences that underlie them are highly practical. The approach is still emerging, and offers at this point more a way of thinking about assessment issues than a blue-print for Monday morning.

What I am suggesting, to use another terminology, is a goal for assessment reform that is implied by our knowledge of the interplay of social inequality and education. This goal is to work out a counter-hegemonic system of assessment; counter-hegemonic in the sense of the criterion of social justice that prioritizes the interests of the least advantaged.

To do this, I emphasize, requires an acknowledgement of the collective dimension of learning, and a concern to assess the collective outcomes of teaching alongside the individual outcomes. Of particular concern, naturally, are the outcomes that might reverse the 'poverty cycles' discussed in Chapter 2 and convert them into cycles of equality.

In thinking these issues through, the experience of education in schools serving the most severely disadvantaged is vital. Yet the scope of action must be, as the issues are, system-wide.

Chapter Seven

Learning From Experience: The Disadvantaged Schools Program

This chapter is based on reports jointly written with Viv White and Ken Johnston, and is published here with their permission.

One of the most enduring of the compensatory education programs discussed in Chapter 2 is the Disadvantaged Schools Program (DSP) in Australia. Little known outside Australia, this is one of the few compensatory education programs to operate on a national scale, and has now been running for eighteen years. It was launched in 1974 by a reforming federal government, and since then has survived several changes of national government, sharp differences at state level, and major changes in general education policy.

By comparison with compensatory education in other countries, the DSP is markedly decentralised in decision-making and democratic in ethos. It has important links with teacher unionism, it emphasises classroom teacher initiative, and it highlights questions of community participation in schools.

From 1987 to 1991 I was a member of a research group working on a national study of the DSP, together with Viv White and Ken Johnston in the core group, and a considerable number of other people working on specific projects. The work was based at a university, funded by the federal government, and therefore formally located outside the school systems. But we set out to open the research as widely as possible to people in the systems, and through interviews, consultations, workshops and networking involved hundreds of teachers, administrators, parents and pupils.

The result is, I think, one of the fullest documentations of a compensatory education program anywhere in the world. The findings are now available, thanks to Deakin University Press, which published the reports of the first round of research in a book called *Running Twice as Hard*, and the Australian Curriculum Studies Association, which published the report of the second round, on assessment and evaluation, in *Measuring Up*.

In this chapter I will discuss parts of the DSP experience that are of particular relevance to fresh attempts to grapple with the issue of education and poverty.

The Program's Design

Issues about social equality in schooling have a long history in Australian education.[1] In understanding the DSP it is important to know that the main resolution of this issue in the past had been an attempt to create large, uniform mass schooling systems. Unlike North American systems, Australian public schools are administered by state governments (equivalent to provincial governments in Canada). There was a vast expansion of the school systems in the 1950s and 1960s, in the context of an industrial boom, and the focus of policy at this time was essentially on providing more and more of the standard-issue schooling.

During the 1960s, however, perceptions about equality were changing. In 1972 the conservative federal government set up a Commission of Enquiry into Poverty which ran for several years and had a high profile. Evidence of stark class inequalities in educational *outcomes* and a reality of far from uniform *provision* had been accumulating since the 1940s. This was suddenly publicised in a widely-discussed book by Tom Roper, *The Myth of Equality*, which pointed to cases like run-down inner-city schools serving immigrant communities; and in a major enquiry into the South Australian education system chaired by Peter Karmel, a liberal economist.[2] The idea that educational equity could be guaranteed by the old tradition of uniform provision was visibly breaking down.

At the end of 1972, twenty-three years of conservative government ended with the victory of the federal Labor Party led by Gough Whitlam. One of the new prime minister's first moves was to bring to Canberra two key authors of the South Australian report, Peter Karmel and Jean Blackburn, as the core of an 'interim committee' to design a program of federal government funding for both state and private schools. Their very influential report *Schools in Australia* set the framework of national education policy for the next two decades.

Part of its argument followed the familiar 'uniform standards' logic, but in two key ways *Schools in Australia* broke with the tradition of uniformity. One was a 'tapering' of the grants to private schools according to economic need, a principle that has survived despite much bickering over the details. The other was a recommendation that the federal government should set up a special program to target both capital and recurrent funds specifically on disadvantaged schools. This was accepted by the government, and the Disadvantaged Schools Program opened for business in 1974.

The idea of a targeted 'poverty program' in education was drawn from the United States and Britain, traditionally the two main sources of ideas for Australian education. From American sources, too, came its main rationale, the idea of cultural difference between the poor and their schools. 'Culture of poverty' and 'linguistic deficit' notions proved very acceptable to Australian educators in the 1970s as an explanation of the facts of disadvantage.

Yet this was not the only agenda in *Schools in Australia*, as Blackburn has pointed out in her recent reflections on policy ideas about disadvantage.[3] The report emphasised, rather, reforming the relationship between schools and poor communities. The Interim Committee rejected the stigmatising implications of 'withdrawal' programs. Concepts of local initiative and community organising were important in the Whitlam government's reform program in social welfare and urban affairs.

And this fitted with developments in teacher unions, where a younger generation of activists was beginning to emphasise questions of participation, social issues and curriculum.

The result of this conjuncture was that the Disadvantaged Schools Program had a framework derived mainly from U.S. poverty programs — it was targeted on a minority (14 per cent) and had 'compensatory' justifications — but also had some distinctive local features. First, it was based on the *school* as its unit of action, not the individual disadvantaged child. The program sought to mobilise the school's community to improve the local educational offerings. Second, it was *teacher-centred*. It relied on teachers currently in disadvantaged schools to generate proposals for the use of funds, and most of the projects funded were actually run by these teachers. Third, it had a distinctly *anti-bureaucratic* ethos. Its activists felt themselves part of a movement to break down the over-centralised, over-controlled, sombre school systems inherited from the colonial past. *Schools in Australia* formulated the revolutionary notion that schools ought to be enjoyed by their pupils, and this was taken seriously as an objective for the DSP.

For the first couple of years there was turmoil as administrators and teachers struggled to turn these ideas into practice. The quality and energy of early DSP projects varied enormously from school to school, depending on the presence of teacher activists and whether the principal blew hot or cool. As our oral history interviews with teachers indicate, the flow of funds initially meant the chance to buy material resources — extra equipment or staffing. For instance:

> Our thinking was originally overwhelmingly about resources — it was class sizes, postage-stamp playgrounds that melted in the sun, and classrooms that were hot and uncomfortable. It all fitted in with something I'd read at university about compensatory education, which at that time was simply interpreted as kids coming from disadvantaged backgrounds. For us at the time, compensatory education translated itself into a differential staffing resource. I was a resource person and so were most of the other people at the time.

Gradually a committee system was built up, within most systems, to administer the federal funds. State and regional committees were set up with some attempt at representativeness. Often a tripartite structure emerged, including nominees of teacher unions, parent organisations, and system administrators. DSP committees were formed in individual schools to write submissions and run projects.

This in itself could represent a major democratisation at school level. As a teacher who worked in one of the first DSP schools recalled:

> The idea that people could be elected to a committee or submit an idea and actually see it funded and then have control over that program to implement it was an enormous morale booster for us.

Within a few years an administrative routine had been created. Equally important, networks of teacher and parent activists were forming around the funding and decision-making structure.

Politics Of The Program

In late 1975 the Whitlam government was thrown out in a constitutional coup and a revived conservative government began to dismantle many Labor programs. The DSP was not touched. But it was not enlarged, though the numbers of children in poverty (by poverty-line measures) rose steeply in the late 1970s and early 1980s.[4] Nor was the program altered very much by the incoming Hawke Labor government after 1983. It has remained at about the same target level (now 16 per cent of the school population), and at about the same relative funding level, between 2 and 3 per cent of federal government expenditure on schools.

The program is about class disadvantage and its class politics are not hard to see. Yet, as often in education, class politics finds a very muted expression in discourse. In an oral history interview one of the parents shrewdly commented on the difficulty of finding a language that is both accurate and politically effective:

> From the beginning it was assumed that it was equality that we were looking for and the issue became, 'How do you get there?' The debate was trying to move away from the compen-

satory notion. It was clear from the beginning that we needed a better form of words because the program is not about compensating for some deficiency. It's about something quite different. But you couldn't talk about the 'working class' and 'class differences.' How could you find a way around that? 'Inequality' was OK but 'class difference' was not OK. To talk about 'poverty' was not all that popular, despite the work of the Poverty Commission. Notions of 'power' and 'empowerment' came much later. I can recall a conference where we invited an academic to speak and I can remember discussions on the State Committee beforehand where we schooled her on what words shouldn't be used because they would antagonise people. I can see that these debates were helpful because they made us think of ways to skirt certain conflicts. But the problem remains. If the program is not about the poor, the small percentage who can't feed themselves, then who is it for? And if you eliminate social class in the analysis, what are you left with?

The federal government set the program up, and the ebb and flow of central support has been important to the grass roots. In the early years the Schools Commission was the key. It supervised the systems in creating the program's structure, Jean Blackburn in particular travelling widely to spread the thinking behind the DSP. Federal government documents were studied intensely at school level to find out what the program was for and how teachers should operate. *Schools in Australia* was known jocularly as 'The Bible.' In the later 1970s the membership of the Schools Commission was changed to reflect the interests of private schools more fully, and philosophical direction of the DSP faltered.

As the program's structures crystallized, marked differences emerged between different states and different systems. In the Victorian government system, parent organisations became very active and the DSP developed a strong identity through state conferences and regional organisation. In the Queensland government system by contrast the DSP was almost invisible. It did not have its first state conference until 1990, after the collapse of a long-entrenched ultra-conservative state government.

In the NSW government system the DSP was relatively decentralised with strong regional committees and active involvement of teacher unionists and parent organisations. In the

South Australian government system it was markedly centralised under a particular administrator who tended to isolate it from the rest of the system.

In the small Northern Territory system the DSP became mainly an Aboriginal education program. In one Catholic system the DSP came under the effective control of a particular order of teaching nuns. In another it was controlled by the diocesan school bureaucracy.

Accordingly, the revival of Schools Commission interest in social justice issues, after the Labor election victory of 1983, faced a much more complex political situation than ten years before. The DSP now meant a range of vested interests and a variety of administrative routines. When the new federal minister of education introduced her main social justice initiative in 1984, it took the form of a new program, the Participation and Equity Program, rather than an expansion of the DSP.[5] The two programs overlapped and competed in embarrassing ways.

There were obvious signs of conflict about the DSP in federal government policymaking circles in the mid 1980s, with activists in the schools increasingly apprehensive about the program's survival. The Schools Commission appointed a committee to conduct a national review of the program in 1984 which reported favourably and recommended continuation. However the minister appointed a committee to review the 'quality and efficiency' of education in Australia as a whole, which took a more economic-rationalist line and recommended that the DSP be a terminating program. The Schools Commission itself replied in a report on special purpose programs, defending its focus on equity.[6]

In relation to the DSP the commission pointed out that the extent of child poverty had risen, and proposed a re-focussing and expansion of the program. Then the Schools Commission was abolished. Its power had plainly been on the wane, and an ambitious new-broom minister, intent on tying education policy more tightly to the government's economic policy, applied the coup de grace. A weaker system of advisory councils now provides little check on ministerial control of funding and administration.

At the same time, however, a broader political logic worked in the program's favour. The Hawke Labor government had drifted to the right since its victory in 1983, provoking periodic explosions of discontent inside the Labor Party on a range of issues from uranium mining and Aboriginal land rights to U.S. missile testing in the Tasman Sea. A climax came when government proposals to shift from a progressive income tax to a consumption tax were embarrassingly defeated, at a 'Tax Summit,' by a coalition of unions and welfare groups.

The government became increasingly concerned to demonstrate to its followers that Labor was still a party of reform, and in 1987-88 a vehicle was found in the idea of 'social justice.' Social Justice Units were set up by the federal government and several state Labor governments, and documents were put out detailing Labor's commitment to social justice across a range of policy areas.[7]

In this context the DSP's position was temporarily strengthened. It was the most obvious example of 'social justice' principles in Australian education policy. In the 1990 election campaign the Labor Party's education statement called the DSP — with some exaggeration — "the cornerstone of the government's commitment to equality of opportunity in education," and promised the first increase in relative scale since 1974.

Turmoil in Canberra was not the only strategic complexity faced by the DSP in the 1980s. The program was about class disadvantage, but did not name class; it named 'disadvantage.' Other forms of disadvantage were coming into focus in education.

Postwar immigration to Australia had created an ethnically diverse workforce which at first attracted little response from the schools. By the end of the 1970s 'multiculturalism' was official policy and a movement for multicultural education developed. The DSP was immediately affected by this, since many schools in poor areas were exactly those with a high proportion of migrant children, especially recent migrants.

In the 1970s the new feminism developed a concern with education. This was registered in an impressive Schools Commission policy document *Girls, School and Society* (1975). Sustained pressure developed for equal opportunity in education and training, and for counter-sexist curricula.

An even more remarkable politicization of the extremely poor Aboriginal community developed. Its most visible campaigns were around land rights for Aboriginal groups in remote areas of the centre and north, but aboriginal groups also became active on education. The DSP, some of whose schools had a high proportion of Aboriginal children, became an important vehicle for this movement.

The DSP, however, had a more ambiguous relationship with the multicultural education movement. The main community leadership was made up of ethnic businessmen and professionals, not the ethnic working class. And the DSP found itself in serious difficulty about gender. Indeed it has never worked out a coherent approach to gender issues, though they have been addressed by projects in individual schools.

Some of these issues crystallized in a debate around the 'Index of Disadvantage.' This is the statistical tool used to identify the most disadvantaged school catchment areas in order to 'target' DSP funds. Its basis is census data broken down by area. This produced two problems. First, the information got out of date between censuses. Some school systems, when they received DSP money from the federal government, abandoned the Index and used their own more current data to identify the most disadvantaged schools.

Second, it was not obvious which of the many possible census variables should be used. Wealth, perhaps the best single guide to class advantage, was not available in the census at all. But a range of other items were: occupation, household income, country of birth, levels of education among adults, size of house, etc.

A complex technical argument about the Index broke out in the mid 1980s.[8] At its core was the question whether the DSP should be specifically focussed on the question of poverty and class disadvantage, or whether its task should be broadened to include any measurable contributor to inequalities in education.

This issue is still unresolved. It has proved difficult because what is at stake is not just a particular interest group's cut of the 'disadvantage' money. There is a deeper issue about the logic of compensatory education.

The DSP's history has been marked by debates about

whether the program is about 'welfare' or about 'education.' At one time DSP funds were used to put social workers into disadvantaged schools, at another time this was rejected on principle. Children coming to school without breakfast make good media stories, and teachers understandably argue that they cannot teach children who are hungry or cold. This was precisely the imagery used in a major campaign on the issue of child poverty mounted by voluntary welfare agencies in 1989-90, under the slogan 'Promise the Children,' a campaign which has helped give legitimacy to the DSP.

But are food and shelter the business of *schools* specifically? A counter argument runs that teachers' business is to teach, and that it is a waste of their expertise and a misuse of schools for them to spend their time doing welfare work. Education cannot compensate for society and it is futile to try.[9]

Along this track, the argument may soon come to deny the educational relevance of *social* disadvantage at all. The school's business is seen as dealing with *educational* disadvantage, defined as below-average performance, slow learning, or something of the kind. 'Compensatory education' then dissolves into remedial teaching, and education is preserved as a depoliticized realm of technical expertise.

So far this position has not been pushed to the point of a rejection of the DSP, though it is easy to see how it could be. Even under a neo-conservative government in NSW at the end of the 1980s, with a spectacularly anti-egalitarian education minister, the DSP continued with relatively little change. Survival, indeed, seemed the keynote of its political history up to the early 1990s.

It could be argued that its survival is connected with the limitations of its design: relatively small scale and narrow targeting. Since the level of child poverty has risen since the DSP began, it would be embarrassing to axe a small program targeted on the neediest pupils. On the other hand positive features of the DSP's design, notably the way it stimulated teacher and parent networks, helped create its own political protection. Education politicians became aware of a 'DSP lobby,' and on occasions both teacher unions and parent organisations have rallied to its defence. One way or another, with its radical origins and ideas, it achieved a considerable legitimacy.

In a changing political and economic climate, however, a program on this scale is also vulnerable. It is too small to show the large quantifiable 'effects' that input/output analysts, in a federal bureaucracy increasingly dominated by conservative economists, demand in program evaluation. A militant new-right government coming in as the Labor hegemony of the 1980s collapses might have nothing to fear from the DSP lobby or indeed any public education interests. So the DSP cannot be regarded as secure.

Participation As Goal And Process

Early thinking in the program identified as a key issue poor children's alienation from school as an institution. The argument sometimes went on to the alienation of parents and teachers too. A teacher activist recalled:

> The DSP started to give people hope. The earlier experience was one of hopelessness. We felt isolated as teachers in our classrooms, isolated from the community and other schools. There was a lot of loneliness around, in the community as well as the school. Kids were generally pushed off to school, they were reluctant attenders. There was a derogatoriness between the staff and a hostility between staff and students. There were a few gags around at the time like, 'There are only two jobs where you are holding people against their will — prison warders and teachers at schools like this.'

The program took on, as one of its major goals, the task of raising levels of participation among all three groups.

This goal was both urgent and ill-defined. No processes were laid down in the program's founding documents for achieving it. As an administrative structure crystallised in the mid and late 1970s, the issue of participation became focussed on the 'submission' mechanism.

Jean Blackburn indicates that it was no part of the Interim Committee's plan that the DSP should be a submission-driven program.[10] Yet that was what it promptly became.

Early submissions were often little more than 'shopping lists' of equipment (books, reading schemes, duplicating

97

machines, etc.) identified by teachers as needed to catch up with better-endowed schools. Alternatively they sought funding for 'enrichment' activities, such as excursions to museums or to national parks, intended to compensate for a presumed cultural deficit in home backgrounds. Even so, the very process of generating submissions and deciding on priorities drew in teachers who otherwise would not have been involved in school policymaking.

> In some ways the DSP wasn't really kids. It was submissions and it was hard yakka [work] and it was the camaraderie of everyone who worked really hard together to get submissions funded. That's where the emphasis was — meeting deadlines and literally writing hundreds of pages of documentation and ringing up firms and getting prices. And it all impinged on our work as classroom teachers at school. And there were battles within the school.

The submission process became the main vehicle for the democratisation of DSP schools. However small the funds were — 'pin money,' as one activist caustically put it — they represented resources available through new channels, outside the traditional authority of school executives [a term covering principal, deputy principals, and in secondary schools heads of departments]. In some schools the DSP Committee, set up to organise the submissions, became a centre of opposition to the executive; in others it operated with the executive's approval or even tacit control.

Whichever was the case, the process expanded the opportunity for classroom teachers to have a voice in school decision making. And this opportunity was often made effective because DSP Committee activists were often also union activists. The teacher unions by and large supported the direction the DSP was taking, and workplace democracy was a theme of unionism in the 1970s. By the end of the decade in some systems (though not all), DSP schools were the leading edge of industrial democracy in Australian education.

The submission process inevitably became a source of conflict. Initially the 'shopping lists' were funded without argument. This was perhaps necessary in the mid 1970s simply to overcome desperate material shortages in the poorest schools.

But this tempted system administrators to treat the DSP as an *alternative* source of funding for equipment rather than an *additional* source. Some barely-concealed scandals about financial manipulation resulted, with systems taking away other sources of funds from the poorest schools to 'balance' their access to federal funds through the DSP.

More openly, it was argued that buying projectors, buying commercial reading programs like DISTAR and SRA, or taking children on excursions, were at best weak and at worst irrelevant responses to the *educational* issues of class and poverty. A demand for 'quality proposals' was formulated, most clearly in the NSW system. In 1977 a project was funded in that state to determine criteria by which funding committees could judge quality. This policy required a tougher surveillance of what schools were doing, by DSP Committees at regional or system level. It implied that eligible schools which submitted proposals judged to be weak might not get funded at all. There were cases where this did in fact happen.

This outcome in turn provoked outrage that some children in poverty should miss out on 'disadvantage' funds simply because their schools had not correctly guessed the priorities of an area committee. An alternative position was argued in favour of 'per capita funding' of eligible schools, leaving to the school all decisions about what to do with the money.

This controversy has continued through the 1980s. 'Per capita funding' has picked up support from those who saw the DSP apparatus itself as a new bureaucracy. 'Submission funding' has been supported by those who feared that under per capita funding, DSP initiatives would dissolve back into routine school management — and with that, the democratic impulse of the program would be lost. We know of schools where just this has happened: DSP funds become a line item in a school budget and only financial administrators can tell which among the school's activities the program is responsible for.

This controversy has been sharpest in the Victorian state system, where it has taken a distinctive turn because of a high level of parent activism. At the time the DSP began, Victoria had the most contested, and in a number of ways the most progressive, of the state education systems. An active interest in curriculum issues was developing inside teacher unions, while parent organisations were becoming increasingly politicised and radical.

In this context the DSP's state and regional committee structure became the vehicle of a significant challenge to teachers' professional monopoly of educational expertise. More than in any other system, DSP funds were used from the early 1980s to employ parents, as well as teachers, as regional consultants. So forceful was this movement that by the late 1980s a backlash among teachers had developed, with bitter arguments about the need for professionalism in the management of the program.

Was this a case of a parent take-over? On the evidence of our survey of teachers, DSP schools in Victoria on average had not even caught up to system-wide norms of parent participation. The teachers answered a nine-item scale about the level of parent participation in a range of school activities. Parents in disadvantaged schools were judged to have a lower level of participation than parents in the rest of the school system.

The finding is hardly surprising. Since DSP schools by definition draw from the most disadvantaged areas, low levels of participation by parents are to be expected.

By the same token, low levels of participation by students are to be expected. On the evidence of the oral history interviews, this was the situation in the early 1970s, with truanting, antagonism to staff, and early leaving the common experience.

But the survey evidence indicates that this situation changed, at least as reported by teachers. The level of student participation in school decision-making was *higher*, to a statistically significant degree, in DSP schools than in the rest of the system.

Though a modest amount of student participation in drawing up submissions has occurred, especially in secondary schools, the submission mechanism is not the focus of participation for students as it has been for teachers and parents. The key mechanism here has been a style of work in DSP *classrooms* which places emphasis on negotiation between teacher and pupils: a participatory pedagogy.

This had roots in the child-centred pedagogy of the progressive education movement which was one of the historical sources of DSP ideas. But it also had more immediate sources in the 1970s in the struggle to create a 'relevant and meaningful' curriculum for working-class children. The academic curriculum, embedded in the old uniform school systems and still hegemonic in Australian schools, was sharply criticized for being abstract in content, over-formal in method, and middle-class in its cultural presuppositions.

A great deal of energy was now put into producing teaching materials that reflected the actual experience of children from working-class, immigrant or Aboriginal, inner-city or remote rural backgrounds. The DSP became a publisher of readers and other texts produced at school level. Through the process of negotiation the pupils themselves became a source of curriculum content in DSP schools. Our survey of Victorian teachers consistently showed DSP teachers relying less than their colleagues in other schools on pre-set curriculum content, such as textbooks, and more on negotiation.

The DSP has not wrought the major change in participation in schools that its founders hoped for. It is simply too small in relation to the issue. It has, however, provided a context for many small-scale gains in participation. And in some settings, when the political conditions were favourable, it has played a part in stimulating systemic change.

Impact On The Curriculum

In Part I of this book I argued for the importance of curriculum issues for social justice in education. What impact has the DSP had on curriculum?

The DSP started at a time when established curricula were more under challenge in Australian education than ever before. Some reform came from inside the systems, such as a renovation of primary mathematics teaching from the late 1950s. Some of it was sponsored by academics, such as a renovation of secondary social science curricula that took shape nationally in the late 1960s. And some came from the student movement of the late 1960s and early 1970s, which challenged the university curricula that legitimated school knowledge, and criticized conventional education as a system of social repression.[11]

These currents all fed into the DSP, though at first their

effect was far from obvious. The program's first preoccupation was the physical restoration of school buildings, playgrounds and equipment, through capital grants and through the 'shopping list' submissions. Early work on curriculum itself had a 'shopping list' flavour, attempting to diversify offerings in schools which had a narrow program. DSP funds put in a remedial reading teacher here, a music program there, an excursion somewhere else.

It was only after three or four years of 'catching up' in physical and to some extent human resources, that arguments about content really began to bite. The demand for 'quality proposals' in NSW in the late 1970s had the effect of focussing discussion on curriculum. An energetic National Coordinator, Shirley Randell, started a monograph series and stirred the systems to document good projects. Both inside and outside the program the idea of 'working class curriculum' was discussed.[12] Though this never became an official concept in program documents, it influenced practice in some schools.

At the same time a counter-offensive against 'progressive education' was being mounted by right-wing press and politicians. Schools generally and progressive education specifically were blamed for youth unemployment and moral decline. 'Standards,' meaning traditional curricula and examinations, were reasserted and a 'back to basics' campaign for spelling, arithmetic, and proper deference to employers was mounted.[13] In the face of such a movement, countenanced (though not vigorously promoted) by a conservative national government, DSP activists by the early 1980s were hardly feeling expansive about curriculum reform.

The substance of what the DSP has done about curriculum is best shown by school-level project documentation. Particular projects are recorded in a wide variety of ways: submissions, accountability reports, conference presentations, newsletters, school-produced curriculum material, and academic studies. In the course of our research we collected approximately 8,000 such documents, and that is only a fraction of the projects undertaken in schools. Obviously it is impossible to illustrate this range of work here. As a bare beginning, to indicate some of the kinds of things done at school level, I have included summaries of five cases in the Appendix: an example of whole-school change; a mathematics room; a conference writing project; aboriginal studies programs; and a pilot project for school-level planning.

The documentation as a whole shows that the bread-and-butter of program activity is language and mathematics skills, particularly language. It is very close to the conventional 'core' in the primary curriculum. This is true of all states and systems.

A radical break from mainstream curriculum could hardly be expected from a program which depends on teachers in the schools, but does not give them enough resources to make major changes in their own jobs. The DSP's design more or less implies that most of its initiatives will be connected with, not at odds with, the usual institutionalized procedures of teaching. This has undoubtedly eased the DSP's acceptance by schools, unions and systems, at the price of limiting its capacity to contest and challenge. Only in settings where the teaching routines are patently in crisis, such as remote Aboriginal communities and some poor multi-ethnic inner-city areas, has curriculum change at school level had a sweeping character.

It was mainly from debates at a policy level that a new curriculum logic emerged. As the number of children in poverty rose in the late 1970s and early 1980s, without a corresponding rise in DSP funding, the problem of the small relative scale of the program became more acute. Criticisms were made of 'add on' projects, where DSP funding simply added an activity to a school's offerings but had no impact on the rest. The goal of DSP work was increasingly formulated as 'whole-school change.' This approach emphasises planning. For instance a school may buy time for teachers and parents to engage in a planning process to renovate the school's language program, or its approach to assessment and certification.

The virtue of this approach is that if successful, it gives leverage to DSP funding. The small DSP funds are used to redesign the use of the much larger recurrent funding the school gets from its system. The weakness is that the idea of 'whole-school change' is in itself content-free. It may be little different from any effective forward planning process, and a kind of forward planning is now becoming common in schools as a result of financial devolution and 'program budgeting.' The idea of planning in itself says nothing specific about questions of social justice in schools, or the needs of working-class or poor children. It is this point which has been picked up in another curriculum debate.

The idea of a 'working class curriculum' led to a dilemma. A separate curriculum might make working class schools more relevant to working class pupils. But — given bourgeois control of universities and certification — it would then lock them into a curriculum ghetto and deny access to higher education. That was what had happened in the old technical schools.

A way past this dilemma might be opened by a broader conception of the 'empowerment' of working-class students as the goal. Such a concept would embrace not only skills and knowledges required for success within the existing system but also skills and knowledges required for collective action to change it. Ideas of this kind were spreading in the DSP in the late 1980s.[14]

The broad picture of curriculum reform through the DSP is much like the picture of teaching practice shown in Chapter 5. Most changes are incremental, and closely tied to existing mainstream curriculum. They have, however, sustained an awareness of the need for broader curriculum reform which can lead to more ambitious proposals.

Strategic Questions

Over its lifetime the DSP has been the venue for some of the most imaginative work in Australian education. Change has been incremental but it has happened.

Being outside the mainstream bureaucracy, the program gave openings for innovation that were hard to come by elsewhere. In certain ways the DSP's own logic has placed DSP schools at the leading edge of change: in industrial democracy, school-based curriculum, goal-based or individualised assessment, participation, multicultural programs, and inter-school networking. In some other fields DSP schools have implemented mainstream system policies ahead of the system as a whole: computer education in one state, three-year planning in another.

Yet there has always been something paradoxical about a 'lighthouse' program based in the most disadvantaged schools. This is where families are poorest, children most often resistant, and teachers faced with severest difficulty. Moral and political ambiguities are evident in the shifting language used, especially in the slides that occur between 'disadvantaged,' 'poor' and 'working class.'

To define the target group of the DSP as 'poor' is substantially correct (though there are always some children in DSP schools who are not poor, and many poor children in other schools). Yet to talk only about poverty is to risk stigmatising the targeted minority. There is evidence that the most disadvantaged 15 per cent at a given time are not culturally distinct, but have a great deal in common with a larger group of working-class families (see Chapter 2). Yet to treat the DSP as simply a 'working class' educational program would be untenable, because the majority of the working class are outside it.

This problem is inherent in the logic of 'poverty programs.' Inequalities in educational access and outcomes, as I showed in Chapter 1, extend across the whole class spectrum. A narrowly targeted program picks out the severest disadvantage and ignores advantage. This procedure obscures the *systemic* nature of the production of disadvantage and advantage. Teachers, researchers and policy makers who know that the issue is about the interplay of education with *class structure as a whole*, like the parent activist quoted above, are caught in a bind so long as educational action is circumscribed by the logic of a poverty program.

The problem can be overcome if the poverty program is part of a larger strategy to address social inequality in education. That was, indeed, the approach of the Interim Committee at the birth of the DSP. Targeted funds to disadvantaged schools supplemented the 'tapering' of the much larger recurrent grants to non-government schools. The weaknesses of this strategy were that it failed to include the very much larger government school systems, which were controlled and funded at state level; and that it failed to address their relationship with the elite private schools.

The result was that no system, state or federal, formulated a policy about class inequalities among the whole array of schools in operation.

The Schools Commission in the mid 1980s had a second chance at a comprehensive equity policy. The DSP figured now as one among an array of special-purpose programs addressing gender, ethnic and rural/urban issues as well as class. The Schools Commission reports *Quality and Equality* (1985) and *In the National Interest* (1987) are a most impressive and sustained defence of equity policy in educational terms. Yet in the political context of the day this was defensive, a reaction to an agenda set by New Right demands for 'efficiency' and small government. The abolition of the commission itself showed the weakness of the position.

A third chance was provided from outside the education system by the emergence of the 'social justice' rhetoric in Labor Party politics. The first statements of these ideas were markedly less coherent than *Quality and Equality* or *Schools in Australia*, being more grab-bags of programs with some equity component than coherent statements of principle or direction. Some critics saw them as basically window-dressing, designed to divert attention from Labor's real abandonment of egalitarian commitments.[15] Yet their language made possible a far-reaching discussion of inequality. In two of the state systems (South Australia and Victoria) substantial work was undertaken to build in 'social justice' as a criterion in policymaking. There is every reason to think that as conservative governments come to power in the 1990s, the leverage this language gave on policy will be lost. (The Victorian Labor government responsible for the assessment reforms discussed in Chapter 6 was defeated in 1992; the Labor governments in South Australia, Western Australia, and Canberra are at best shaky.)

The DSP succeeded, as few other initiatives in Australian education have, in tapping the energy and inventiveness of classroom teachers and parents. It managed not only to mobilize a great deal of local action but also to sustain it over a decade and a half of erratic support from the centre. The decentralised design of the program has been crucial in this.

Yet the marked decentralization of initiative and control,

firstly to the thirteen systems and secondly to the regions and schools, has carried costs. It is sometimes remarked that the DSP is not one program but thirteen. There is little coordination between the systems, and there has certainly been no attempt at concerted action on a national scale.

Our visits and interviews around the program found a great deal of ignorance (as well as keen curiosity) about what was going on in other states, and even within states about what was going on in other areas. Under one national coordinator a push was made to circulate information and experience; this died away in the early 1980s. With the demise of the Schools Commission, federal government initiative in the program sank to a historic low. Between 1985 and 1991 three separate reports recommended beefing up the centre's capacity to document and circulate information around the program, a fairly cheap reform, but this advice was ignored. In 1989 one of the state systems, in the absence of federal action, took the initiative and called a national conference on poverty and education — to which the federal authorities failed to come. In 1990 teacher unions and welfare organisations, picking up the child poverty issue, called a summit conference on the same theme; again the initiative came from outside the federal administration.

The problem is, perhaps, that an existing poverty program may be embarrassing to dismantle but carries few positive benefits for a government. Whatever the commitment of individual administrators — and there are certainly people in the education hierarchy who care about social justice — there is little political incentive for a government to stick with the difficult incremental business of improving a program in being.

The DSP in Australia has a number of implications for work on poverty and education in other countries. The story emphasises the inherently political character of special-purpose programs. There is no technical solution to problems of inequality. There is, rather, a range of ways in which the groups and interests at stake can be addressed and connected through schooling. The terms on which these connections are made will shape the kind of 'output' the program provides.

The DSP highlights a crucially important question for educational reforms: who will implement them, and in what settings? The success the DSP has had is largely due to one of its unintended effects, the creation of an informal network of teacher and community activists (Chapter 5). Ways of building and resourcing such networks should be a key issue in designing reforms.

The DSP shows both the virtues and the limits of a decentralised program. A great deal of scope is provided for local initiative, and when things go well this produces imaginative work carefully tailored to local needs. But the small scale of a special-purpose program limits the impact of such work, and decentralisation also means a lack of coordinated work on what are, after all, large-scale social and educational problems. The DSP has reached the point where curriculum reform on a large scale is on the agenda; but this larger change is very difficult to get started.

As this suggests, the articulation between special-purpose reform programs and the systems in which they operate is a vital issue. To the extent a program is encapsulated, or over-shadowed and assimilated, its impact will be lost, however well designed it may be. Ways in which practice generated in a program, especially on curriculum issues, can be moved out into the forum of a whole education system, are key questions if we are to improve the dismal record of Western education systems in serving children in poverty.

Chapter Eight

Work For Researchers

Paradigms Of Knowledge
And Practicalities Of Research

Research is the process of producing knowledge, thus a kind of industry. There is a labour process: what researchers do. There is a workforce: who researchers are. There is a distribution and consumption process: how the knowledge is circulated, and how it gets used.

The sociology of knowledge, a discipline more often honoured in the spirit than practised in the flesh, tells us that these processes are shaped by institutional and cultural structures. Knowledge is a social product not in a vague metaphysical sense, but in hard and intrusive detail. What is known, by whom, about whom, with what effects — these are social, indeed political, questions.

To say this is not to say, as some skeptical epistemologists do, that *truth* is eliminated as an issue, or becomes an effect of power. I don't go all the way with Foucault; I think that truth is in many circumstances a subversive force that disrupts power/knowledge regimes. (If it were not, we would not see so much energy expended by governments and corporations in controlling knowledge.)

But Michel Foucault's investigations, and those of the feminist epistemologists like Susan Bordo and Evelyn Keller who have recently and stunningly displayed the gender sub-text in the hardest of 'hard' science, should alert us to the social underpinnings of different paradigms of knowledge. Thomas Kuhn made us familiar with the idea that knowledge in a given field may be organised in different and incompatible ways, according to rival 'paradigms.' We now need to connect this insight, more firmly than Kuhn and the philosophers have been able to do, with the analysis of research as a production process, and with the consumption of its products.[1]

There are, as I argued in Chapter 3, social options for the organisation of any field of knowledge at a given time. Which possibilities for the organisation of the knowledge-production process are realised in research practice is, at one and the same time, an epistemological and a political issue. Researchers make choices about the making of knowledge, but the choices are not innocent, and are never simply technical.

Three Types Of Educational Knowledge And Research

(1) *Positivist*. The dominant style of educational research at present has the aspiration of creating a scientific basis for educational practice. The highest prestige is accorded to 'basic' or 'fundamental' research intended to advance this science. The methods of highest prestige are controlled experiment, or statistical analysis that approximates experimental control. Science itself is understood through a positivist epistemology, as the production of empirically-based generalisations which, after testing and and verification, can be 'applied' by practitioners.

This positivist model is hegemonic in Western-style education systems, providing the common-sense background to most discussions of research. It provides the groundwork, for instance, for the familiar distinction between 'basic' and 'applied' research.

The institutional bases of positivist research are the universities and research institutes. Its rise to dominance in educational discourse was intimately bound up with the growth of a professionalized research workforce — produced by graduate departments of education and psychology (and to a lesser extent sociology, economics, statistics); employed by universities on research grants, by research institutes, or by research offices in education systems. A high level of specialised training is required particularly by the formal measurement procedures and statistical analysis that are central features of the research style.

Positivist epistemology, professional training and institutional base combine to produce a high level of abstraction in the research. This is not an error or an aberration, it is inherent in the goal of an educational science based on the broadest possible generalisations. It is characteristic of papers in educational research journals to frame their conclusions in universalized terms, about 'learning,' 'resources,' or 'instruction' in general. It is quite common in journal articles that the exact time and place of the research goes unreported, so unimportant is concrete detail considered.

With this abstraction goes a sharp separation between the producers and consumers of knowledge. School teachers do not research, while researchers do not teach in schools. (Though many researchers have been teachers at an earlier stage of their careers.)

School teachers do not have much say in all this, as they do not fund the research. But governments do, and in this relation lies one of the key difficulties about positivist research. The ambition to produce a generalized science is at odds with the practical demands of running an education system. For this, administrations mostly need particular, local information: the demographic projections for a given region, the training and skills of a teaching workforce, the pattern of subject choice, the current state of the curriculum.

Administrators in their offices (like teachers in their classrooms) mostly have a perfectly good practical knowledge of how to run a school system. They do not need an abstract science of education (or of management, for that matter) to tell them what to do. Hence their often-expressed irritation at the irrelevance or uselessness of most of the knowledge produced by academics in the name of 'basic' research. Hence periodic attempts to use the financial power of governments to re-mould the production of knowledge closer to the practitioners' desire.

The case of Australia is reasonably typical. In the 1970s the federal government put education research funds into an Education Research and Development Committee. Education was then the only academic field to have its 'research' funds specifically designated R&D. In the late 1980s a much broader attempt was made to organize all public research funding around designated 'national goals.' This provoked fierce complaints from the universities about an attack on academic freedom. Significant amounts of new education research money were kept out of even this re-vamped research granting structure and put directly into government-commissioned projects.

(2) *Quick-and-Dirty*. Given all this, it is not surprising that another genre of research has grown up to meet the needs of educational administrators and policymakers. This does not challenge positivism so much as sit beside it in the spaces positivism does not fit. It has no well-recognised name. Following the pungent description of a practitioner, I will call it QAD research, for 'quick-and-dirty' data-gathering.

QAD research probably accounts for at least as much data-gathering activity as positivist educational science, though it is harder to measure and account for since most of its results are never published. Its institutional base is the administrative apparatus that runs education systems: ministries, regional offices, local boards, principals' offices.

Its workforce is mainly the administrators themselves (often the second-echelon administrators who are delegated by unit heads to 'get the facts' on such-and-such an issue). They are sometimes assisted by professional researchers from a departmental research office or a research institute, but most often do the job themselves, using their background knowledge of the education system they work in, and some rough-and-ready ideas of research practice.

When head office sends out a form to be filled in by the regions, or the regional office tallies up the schools offering such-and-such a program, or a principal decides to send a survey home to parents, this is QAD research. Its methods include shorthand versions of positivist research methods, e.g. quickly-constructed questionnaires sent out with little or no pre-testing.

But they also include data-gathering techniques quite inadmissible in the academic approach, such as calling some knowledgeable person on the telephone and asking her what the score is.

Sometimes academics are called upon to do this kind of research, as I have been, and they are likely to find the experience disconcerting, if not distressing. The time-frame in QAD research is likely to be weeks, where in academic education science the time-frame is measured in years. One would still be pre-testing the instruments for an academic study at the time a QAD study is all wrapped up and the policy decisions are history.

An academic is likely to see this as undue haste producing research of poor quality; but I want to suggest another view. QAD is a knowledge production process organised on different institutional bases and from a different point of view. The research can be perfectly 'good' with respect to the institutional practice in which it is used, though it is no good at all from the perspective of producing a generalised science.

The real problems it raises are about the shaping of the administrative agendas to which QAD responds, and the control and distribution of the knowledge produced. For 'administration' is no more a disembodied technical process than 'research' is. It has its own politics. As Anna Yeatman and Michael Pusey have recently shown for the Australian case,[2] reform agendas moving through bureaucracies can re-shape conceptions of problems, and available solutions, quite dramatically. The recent impact of the ideology of 'economic rationalism' on educational policy-making in Australia is a striking example of how disputable administrative common sense can be.

(3) *Teacher-based.* Classroom teachers have no place in most research agendas. Teachers are of course the *objects* of positivist research, in a body of work on teaching styles, instructional methods, etc. (Strictly speaking, teachers as persons and as workers are not the objects of this research, rather they are the bearers of the *variables* which are the true objects of knowledge.)

But teachers are not the authors of positivist research,

except when they step outside their classroom jobs and sign up for MEd or PhD theses. And they are not usually the authors of QAD research, except when they are promoted out of the classroom to administer schools or to chair committees.

This absence from research agendas reflects the usual view of teachers, which sees their work basically as *implementing* something decided elsewhere — whether 'scientific' conclusions about instruction, or system prescriptions for curriculum, or societal values. In this view teachers *consume* research knowledge, as validated by academics or in the form of administrative decisions, but have no other relationship to research.

But if we take a more industrially realistic view of teachers, as proposed in Chapter 5, and investigate their actual labour process and the social conditions that shape it, then a different relation to knowledge appears.

In the nature of their work, teachers gather a great deal of knowledge. Part of this is curriculum knowledge. Syllabuses and other curriculum documents, however expertly prepared, can only be guides. Like the famous cookery book that presupposes someone who knows how to cook, curriculum documents presuppose someone who knows how to teach. 'Knowing how to teach' includes having methods for expanding documentary guidelines into day-by-day, minute-by-minute sequences of interaction. Assembling materials, finding relevant examples, finding connections between different items and types of knowledge, are all part of teachers' everyday work.

Another part of the knowledge teachers gather is about their pupils: styles of learning, levels of information, current skills, motives and emotions, friendships, family backgrounds, personal problems, and so on. Most of this information is gathered on the run in the everyday work of the classroom. Sometimes this is supplemented by more formal procedures of assessment and evaluation, depending on the micro-technologies available in the school, and the time and energy available to use them.

In more formal terms, what we see here is a knowledge-production process that is reflexively integrated into the practice of teaching. Teachers discover and produce relevant knowledge in an ongoing way in the course of their labour process.

For the most part this is an un-named and un-theorised process. It is not called 'research' and (except in the shape of formal assessment of pupils) is not much discussed in teacher training.

At times, however, it can become more visible; and this is most likely to happen when a group of teachers are facing a situation that calls in question many of the routines of teaching. Such a situation is teaching in a context of severe poverty. In this case a conscious, joint process of producing and discussing practice-relevant knowledge may develop at school level.

An example is the Martin Street school discussed in the Appendix. In this school the staff came to an agreement that a renovation of the school's assessment system was needed; but there were few available guidelines for doing that. So they appointed one of the teachers in the school as their researcher to gather publications, models, experience from other schools, and make links with academics and administrators — feeding all this back into the continuing discussions and trials going on in the school.

The Research Workforce

The most visible component of the research workforce for educational science is the academic staff (in North American terms, faculty) of universities. The conditions of work in universities are highly relevant to the kind of research that comes out of them.

The academic career path is open mainly to people who are able to produce a stream of research reports in refereed journals, or books which are well reviewed in such journals. Reviewing and refereeing are accountability mechanisms which tie the work of academics in to the scrutiny of other academics, and heavily discount the worth of work in other forums. Anyone who has sat on an academic appointment or promotion committee, and has heard the devastating effect of epithets like 'journalistic,' 'anecdotal,' or 'impressionistic,' will know what I mean. In the case of education studies, these mechanisms establish the hegemony of positivist knowledge production over any other kind.

I do not wish to open the door to academic-bashing; there are good reasons why academic work should have a high degree of autonomy. We should also bear in mind that many education academics have been school teachers and administrators, and have a personal awareness of the issues faced by teachers and administrators. Education studies do not float free.

Nevertheless academic autonomy — realised in a context of career-making, with the particular economy of university life (notably its lack of support services and its striking lack of long-term guarantees of resources), and with the hegemony of positivist models of knowledge — pushes strongly towards an abstracted conception and practice of research.

To criticize this weakness in education research is easy; but how can it be overcome without destroying the capacity for independent analysis which is the main point of having a university in the first place? The problem has no instant solutions. However I think two directions are clear.

First, we need research funding structures that encourage links between particular groups of academics and particular groups of schools, especially long-term links. This could key research in more closely to the developing practical issues at the chalk face, and give teachers a greater chance to set research agendas.

Second, we need to address the question of publication and recognition of academic work. The vehicles for academically-respected, career-relevant publication are in fact very narrow. (This book, for instance, will not advance my academic career: too 'journalistic.') There are many academic journals, but mostly of the same kind, mostly with very small circulations, mostly with no readership among teachers and no impact on policy makers.

I think these unfortunate conditions for recognition of research among academics can be changed, if vehicles are created which provide for scrutiny and testing of the research in practice by practitioners, as well as by other academic researchers. A diversification (rather than a simple multiplication) of channels is needed. I would argue that a designated part of public research budgets should be invested in 'dissemination,' in the creation and development of means of communication of and about research.

For another key part of the research workforce, the main problem is not recognition and advancement but survival. Most of the research labour done in universities, and in many research institutes, is done by temporary workers on 'soft money': graduate students, part-time research assistants, fixed-term contract employees.

These are the people on the factory floor of research, who do most of the personal contact, live on the job, and gather most of the tacit knowledge about what is really going on. Rough stability in overall education research budgets means that there is always a certain volume of this work available. But the parcelling-out of most of this budget from year to year on a project-by-project basis means massive instability and uncertainty for individual workers. They are dependent for offers of work on academics or research administrators who have budgets; research assistants do not themselves apply for research grants and would not get them if they did.

We must acknowledge that a key part of the research workforce operates under appalling industrial conditions, with frequent changes of task and supervision, with no job security, and no clear career path. This is not exactly likely to encourage bold, creative and independent thinking.

Our research funding practices produce the paradoxical effect that the part of the workforce which is most likely to have intimate practical knowledge of the production of knowledge, is least likely to influence the planning and design of research, and has no incentive at all to think about research in a long-term way.

I think this is one of the key mechanisms depressing the quality of professional research, and that it urgently needs attention. Individual institutions (e.g. particular university departments) often try to do something about it locally. For instance, they try to make sure research staff have a regular flow of offers of work.

But the issue is much larger and needs to be addressed at the policy level. The best sources of ideas, information and practical solutions on these issues are the unions covering research staff. Accordingly, research policy making structures should automatically include these unions on a permanent basis.

For yet another part of the workforce, school teachers, the problem is getting the research element of their work recognised at all. Industrial agreements specify preparation time, and that is about as close as it usually gets. Research training is not normally part of teacher training programs, let alone research reporting.

Yet teachers are producers as well as consumers of knowledge. They are particularly important producers in relation to the renovation of education, since teachers are key actors in school reform and their production of knowledge is so closely connected to teaching practice. Therefore a comprehensive research policy needs to give thought to how teachers can be developed as researchers, what kind of support they need, and how their work can be circulated and scrutinised.

It helps to consider the school as a research community and to ask how the school as an institution can be made more effective in this role. At present, the knowledge teachers acquire often goes no further than their own classrooms. One of the key moves, then, is to create forums where this knowledge can circulate, and to organise schedules to make this circulation possible. The minute-to-minute daily pressure of classroom teaching is a powerful constraint on teachers' capacity to organise and circulate their knowledge. The assessment research at Martin Street school, described in the Appenix, addressed exactly this problem.

The 'barefoot doctor' model of research worked out at Martin Street has in my view great potential. It is flexible, can be short or long term, and can be applied to an enormous range of problems. It locates the production of knowledge close to the point where it will be used.

But to realise this potential the approach needs to be supported at system level, and by professional researchers. Research funding structures need to be created that can be accessed by schools, and practical support must come with the funds. Frameworks and procedures need to be thought through. Positivist research paradigms are of little use — may even be counter-productive, as they set up norms that are impossible to realise in the practicalities of school life. The models of most relevance are the methods of reflexive community research that have been developed in welfare, social policy and community health. Readable accounts of these methods exist, especially the pioneering books written by Yoland Wadsworth, and deserve to be widely known among educators.[3]

Finally we need to consider how teacher-produced knowledge can be circulated between schools, as well as within them; and how it can be subjected to scrutiny and debate. I take such scrutiny to be an essential component of any knowledge-creation process that is trying to do more than reproduce traditional ideas — scrutiny is an essential component of both science and social critique.[4]

This will not readily happen in conventional research forums (though I would certainly favour opening up academic journals more to the work of teachers). There is perhaps more potential in the kind of publication that already has an audience among teachers around issues of practice, ranging from union journals through subject association magazines to system gazettes and general-purpose magazines. Some teacher research is already published in these media, and *Our Schools/ Our Selves* can take legitimate pride in its contribution to this process.

Democratising Research

The abstractness and narrowness that plague education research can be overcome, though the task is not an easy one. It will be helped, I think, by having well-worked-out models of what a more democratic research practice would be.

A notable example is what Wadsworth calls participatory action research (PAR). Built on a reflexive rather than a positivist epistemology, PAR starts with a group (e.g. a school, a community organisation, a group of health educators) and works from their actual practice to define their needs for knowledge.

PAR then seeks to mobilise and expand the group's own capacities for research, to build data-gathering and interpretation into the group's own work. It tries to set up direct and continuing feedback between practice and research.

If this sounds like a prescription for amateurism, it is not. Professional researchers are involved in setting up the process, in the design and conduct of the work. But their relationship to the groups involved is different from the Researcher/Subject or Researcher/Consumer relation in conventional research models.

Decisions are made by negotiation between specialist researchers and the 'critical reference group,' as Wadsworth calls it. The researcher functions to a large extent as a community educator, disseminating her expertise as widely as possible. When the results of the research are compiled, the primary audience to be addressed is the critical reference group (and other people in a similar situation), so the form of reporting is shaped by the practice involved.

This general approach allows for wide variation in the scale of research, in the details of the relationship between professionals and critical reference group, and in the ways research is linked to practice. PAR shades off into a wider range of research approaches that try to break down the researcher/researched divide and democratise the consumption of research.

I do not mean to suggest that research of this kind is exactly trouble-free. My own experience of community-based education research (in AIDS prevention education) posed awkward enough problems. Professional researchers' needs to have a body of data thoroughly analyzed, clash with community educators' needs for quick guidance, however imperfect. Future research funding depends on academic credibility, which in turn depends on academic publications; but producing academic publications is very time-consuming and is a distraction when the priority is to get results urgently into the hands of non-academic users. Connecting community-generated research to governmental policymaking is difficult.[5]

Yet these problems can be managed, and community-controlled research of good quality, as well as practical use, can be produced. Reflecting on these issues, and on other experiences with participatory research, I would raise two main issues about the support structures needed to develop participatory research on a wider scale.

The first concerns decentralised research funding. To stimulate a broad spectrum of participatory research projects requires a broad distribution of funds, and a relaxation of central control over their awarding and use. The AIDS project just mentioned was exceptional in its scale and cost. Most participatory action projects are, as research costs go, granter-friendly.

But broad distribution of relatively small grants goes against the grain of many funding bodies. Certainly the trend in Australian research policy in recent years has been in exactly the opposite direction: larger grants on a more selective basis, supposedly supporting 'excellence.'

We should therefore look with skeptical eyes at the assumptions about the knowledge-production process that are built into research administration at present. In my view they often reflect mistaken — though given the hierarchical organisation of academic life, understandable — views about how knowledge is developed as a whole. The 'great man' theory of history, long obsolete elsewhere, has an odd currency in the research world — sustained by such carnivals as the Nobel Prizes and the cult of 'first publication.' (Why first publication, rather than deepest understanding, should be valued by a group of intellectuals is a disturbing question.)

A decentralised approach to research funding would be better adapted to the advancement of knowledge and encouragement of innovation across a broad front. In my view this is closer to how knowledge (including natural-science knowledge) generally develops, and is certainly better adapted to supporting teacher-initiated research agendas. It assumes that useful ideas and discoveries are likely to arise from many points, once there is encouragement to pursue research and reflection.

But for this to turn into systematic and public knowledge, subject to testing, critique and development, another condition is required: an adequate *dissemination system*. As I have already suggested, this is a crucial weakness in current research structures. Academic research usually does not reach the people who should ultimately use it. School-level needs do not easily translate into academic research agendas. QAD findings do not get into public arenas. And teachers' knowledge often stays in one classroom or at best in one staffroom.

Dissemination is too important to remain as unplanned, as

unsupported, and as untheorised as it now is. Indeed the term 'dissemination' itself is inadequate, implying a one-way flow of information and authoritative instruction. What we need, rather, is a multiplicity of *forums* for the circulation of ideas and information.

We should take serious note of the skills and resources needed for running such forums. I would argue, specifically, that there is an important role for *journalists* in the circulation of educational research, people who are trained and experienced in the communication of events and ideas to non-technical audiences. I suggest therefore that research budgets should routinely provide for the employment of journalists as part of the research workforce.

Journalists are often employed by universities and government agencies at present, and often write about research in the course of that work, but principally in a *public-relations* function for the institution — trying to convey how impressive its research activities are. This is, to say the least, an inadequate use of journalists' skills. There should be an *organic* role for journalists in the creation of a widespread research community in education systems, in the generation of dialogue and reflection, as well as in the celebration of achievements.

What I am suggesting is that we need to problematise what is usually taken for granted in research reporting: who is the audience, how they will use the communication, what is the relation between the parties to the communication.

In participatory action research, it is important that the process of communication should stretch beyond the initial 'critical reference group' to others in similar or related situations. There is a task here for central funding agencies, as the community groups involved in PAR rarely have the resources or the public profile to achieve this by themselves. One can see here a clear role for research journalism, funded centrally but provided as a service to local groups, and feeding information out through a variety of print, electronic and other media.

Having ladled out the optimism, I must finish on a darker note. The world of educational research is all too well protected, and our professional talk within it is all too bland. I realise I have mentioned an AIDS research program without reference to what the people in it were going through: deadly illness, bereavement and social threat. Research on poverty and education likewise is not a topic for the faint-hearted; one is dealing much of the time with damaged lives, with situations of oppression and violence, with degraded and sometimes disgusting environments, and one is conscious all the time of the awful silence of the rich.

Education systems serve both as a means of enlightenment and cultural advance, and as a means of social exclusion and oppression. That is the paradox with which educational sociology continually grapples. It is documented in all the statistics of class selectiveness, of ethnic segregation, of gender inequalities. But it is rare that the human realities beneath these statistics are thematised in publicly funded education research.

For these realities, one turns rather to texts on the margins of education research, with no diplomatic standing, so to speak. I mean works like Richard Sennett and Jonathan Cobb's *The Hidden Injuries of Class*, documenting the emotional disruption of working-class families around the promise of advancement through education; or Jonathan Kozol's scarring books about schooling, racism and poverty, *Death at an Early Age* and *Savage Inequalities*; or John Embling's *Fragmented Lives*, about youth who hardly get to school at all. Such works get to the level of reality they do by ignoring our canons of proper research method. (That such studies come — in the case of Sennett and Cobb, and Kozol — from the wealthiest country on earth, in the shadow of the largest and richest university system, makes them all the more poignant.)

What kind of research would be useful to a black teenager facing crack and structural unemployment in a Boston apartment, or under the smog in Los Angeles? What research would be useful to a Hamilton youth staring at those shrinking steelworks, or a bunch of kids in Alberta wondering where the oil jobs went? Probably nothing that looks very much like the 'education research' that universities and governments are currently doing.

What kind of research, for that matter, would be useful to an illiterate villager in India? Or an illiterate city-dweller in Australia? The kind of research that might be useful to them, or to educators working directly with them, is not necessarily the kind of research that education authorities want to have. It would be deeply uncomfortable research, because it would illuminate the failures, the injustices, and the reactionary trends in education systems.

The fact that critical research is nevertheless done is a tribute to the mixed motives of education authorities: genuine concern for truth and justice does coexist with conservatism, careerism and defensiveness. If we are to expand the chances of research supporting the educational interests of the excluded, we must take thought about how to provide political protection for education authorities against the political or bureaucratic fall-out from following their concern for truth and justice.

Here, I think, the politics of research must be addressed in a broader political context. The issue must be taken up by groups who normally leave 'research' as a technical issue to the experts — groups like teacher unions, parent organisations, ethnic and community coalitions. There is only so much that can be done to improve education research from inside the institutional whale. In the long run, the quality of educational thought and investigation will reflect the quality of democracy in the society as a whole.

Appendix

Examples Of Practice In Disadvantaged Schools

I: School-Based Assessment Renovations

These two case studies are adapted from R. W. Connell, K. M. Johnston and V. M. White, *Measuring Up*, Australian Curriculum Studies Association, 1992; further cases are discussed in that report.

1. A Whole-School Strategy

Martin Street Primary School is set on a tongue of suburb between paddocks, railway, highway and waste land. The area is an established suburb, by urban fringe standards; houses on smallish blocks, about half of them fibro, half a mixture of brick veneer and cladding. In the early 1980s the school itself was all demountables, but these have largely been replaced by new, well designed buildings. The enrollment of the school has fallen from a peak of 900 to around 650 as the population of this largely working class area has aged.

Three years ago a group of senior staff, concerned about the general problem of discipline and low staff morale, set about the process of change. According to the Deputy, whose energy provided an impetus for action, a firmer discipline regime, while desirable, would not solve the problem in any fundamental sense. The real difficulty was the "mismatch of curriculum."

Curriculum thus became the focus of a renovation process at Martin Street. The staff began with the language area and used DSP funds to revamp their program. Assessment only became an item on the agenda for school discussion when it became clear that there was a discrepancy between the new language arts strategies and the old assessment practices. Towards the end of the second year of the renovation, the staff met together in a workshop to discuss the plan of action on this issue. They decided to apply for DSP funds to employ a full-time person to work as a staff development agent. The submission was successful and a senior teacher was freed from classroom duties to carry forward the task of assessment reform.

The teacher appointed scoured the countryside for resources and assistance, finding little guidance but managing to collect a range of assessment "tools." In the first half of the third year of reform she worked with staff in trying out the various assessment tools and strategies in the classroom. In the middle of the third year, the staff met together for another assessment workshop. This time they pooled their experiences of the different techniques that they had been trialling, and developed consensus about which ones to adopt across the school.

As a result of this process, the staff at Martin Street have come up with a particular conception of "good assessment practice." The mandatory element for all classroom teachers is the *pupil profile*. The profile is a record of the individual child's performance (in the language area especially), and it consists of samples of work, anecdotal records of teacher observations and comments. The profiles become an ongoing descriptive record of the children's progress. They accompany the children as they go from teacher to teacher through the school.

A second technique, the *language interview*, has a more diagnostic flavour. In effect, half hour tutorial sessions are arranged with each student in a class over a cycle of about four weeks, from which the teacher develops an individual program of diagnostic work.

A third technique links assessment with reporting to parents.

The staff decided that the first four weeks of every year would not be programmed but devoted to the *observation* of the children. At the end of that period, they would meet the parents to discuss individual children. The year's program would be developed to build on the knowledge so gained and it would be monitored and adjusted as a result of observation and testing throughout the year.

2. Diffusion From One Department

Secondary schools are organizationally more complex, and both their greater bureaucratization and their closer link to credentialling make them harder to renovate. Nevertheless, some are moving in the same direction as Martin Street Primary.

At Wells High School the original site of change was the English/History faculty, and the driving forces were two teachers in particular. Stephen who taught English was also the DSP chairperson, while Maria was responsible for Language Across the Curriculum. Stephen had come across new ideas about assessment through his professional reading in the English area. He became more sure of his ideas when he joined the local DSP committee and helped plan staff development workshops on such themes as inquiry learning, cooperative classrooms and strategies of teaching and learning. With the support of the head teacher in English, he trialled descriptive assessment and profiling in his own English class. For him it worked, and he was able to persuade his colleagues in the faculty to adopt the new regime the following year.

The system is comparatively simple. Along with any assessment task, the students are also given the criteria that the teacher will use to evaluate the work. Depending on the task, the teacher will describe specific writing skills, reading skills, speaking skills or listening skills. When they come to evaluate the work, they write descriptive comments on an assessment sheet about how well the student has met the criteria. This assessment sheet is returned to the student, but a copy is attached to their Profile Sheet.

The purpose of the Profile Sheet is to keep a cumulative summary of comments from the assessment sheets as they build up over the year. Teachers are also encouraged to include on the Profile Sheet any relevant observations about the student's classroom participation.

From the point of view of learning and teaching, this system is a great improvement upon the conventional assessment regime. Maria pointed out the benefits for the students.

> We are getting good results. One, the kids' interest in English has increased just incredibly. Two, there are improvements in skills that we can see developing. And three, it just seems to make English more fun. Kids know what they have to do. Everything is clearly defined for them and they can think, "Well, to the best of my ability I am going to meet these criteria." And also because we don't have competition. I'm not worried about what the next bloke is doing. We have a far more cooperative classroom in that the kids will proof-read each other's work. They'll say, "Look, why don't you put this in?" There's no feeling that if I give something of myself away to another person then I am disadvantaging myself. There is no reason why kids shouldn't feel good about what they can do rather than what they can't. Feeling a limited success is much better than feeling a total failure.

The problem at Wells High is how to break the walls that insulate the other faculties from these changes. The barriers are partly organizational; the strong faculty divisions block the spread of ideas and innovations. But there are also mental barriers that get in the way. There is a tendency among the Mathematics and Science staff, for example, to exempt their subject from the new assessment regime on the grounds that it is a qualitatively different kind of knowledge, more highly structured and based on content rather than skills.

There are signs, however, that the new approach is spreading beyond the English faculty at Wells High. Almost half the teaching staff have now attended the DSP workshops on effective learning and here and there small cracks are visible. Maria, as the Language Across the Curriculum teacher, is one of the few people in the school who can legitimately work across faculty lines. She has transplanted ideas and techniques that have been trialled in the English domain into new soil.

II. School-Level Curriculum And Planning Projects

These case studies are condensed from Chapter 5 of R. W. Connell, V. M. White and K. M. Johnston, *Running Twice as Hard*, Geelong, Geelong University Press, 1991; 54 other cases are given in that report.

1. 'A Slow Miracle': Gradual Institutional Change

Invermay Primary School (Tasmania) has attempted to document the whole process of change over a four-year period from the time it came on the program. The major initial concerns are identified as well as the factors which have resulted in successful change. The primary needs of the school were identified as improvement in the reading ability of the children and in the school environment. Initiatives taken were to seek funds from the program for remedial teachers in reading and maths; and the principal making changes to the 'climate' of the school by abandoning corporal punishment and increasing support for teachers by seeking their advice and assisting their professional development. Later, the school's language program was transformed to involve the whole school. The necessity for teachers to communicate more closely with the parents of the children was also recognised. The school's library was built up as part of the language program and over the years sporting equipment and playground improvements were also purchased through DSP submissions.

2. The Mathematics Room

A renovation of mathematics in an outer metropolitan primary school in Western Australia began with two college lecturers assisting with 'placement tests' which showed a wide range of achievement in each grade. Teachers were then supplied with a wide range of materials and resources. 'Maths had to be meaningful and enjoyable.' A maths room was established as a base for a 'learning by doing' program, well equipped with resources, texts and games. This centralization allowed maximum use of resources. Results reported include: improved small group work, placement tests and evaluations carried out in 1980 to 1983 have all shown a steadily increasing rate of practical maths sessions taken by all teachers. There has also been an increased level of achievement in maths by children in all year levels. In some cases, the increased level of achievement has been considerable.

The setting up of a maths room in which groups of students work with practical, concrete materials appears frequently in reports; some secondary schools have them too. Maths projects mainly concentrate on giving students more hands on practical experience.

3. Conference Writing

Thirty-two adults including parents, teachers and aides participate in this scheme, introduced in a suburban primary school in Western Australia. It allows up to eight people to be involved with each Year Level (Years 1, 2 and 3) of approximately 50 children on a daily basis. Three areas of the school are used and the children move to these areas immediately after the morning fitness programme. The writing session runs from 9:15 am to 9:45 am each day. Two teachers conference each year level while others move around helping the children with their work.

Approximately one in every four stories done by a child is 'conferenced' and this work is then published. The work is typed and made into booklets. Room is left on each page for illustrations to be done by the children. Teacher aides and parents help out with the typing and making of books. Parents were in-serviced by the Language Advisor at the commencement of the year. The school has a District Remedial Class and these children and their teacher take part in the program.

Results: Generally there appears to be a very positive attitude towards the program by children, parents and teachers. There is still room in which further development can be made, particularly in relation to child editing and conference questioning techniques. The area of stimulating children in the writing of their stories is one which can also be further developed. Anecdotal records kept by the teachers on all children who are 'conferenced' enable progress to be carefully monitored.

Comment by teacher: "I feel that there are two important

factors which have contributed to what I consider to be a quite successful approach to writing. Because we are an open area school we can arrange very flexible seating arrangements and teachers and parents can move quite freely between areas. The second factor is the amount of support we have been able to provide in the form of personnel and money for both hardware and software materials through the Priority Schools Program [i.e. the DSP]."

4. Aboriginal Studies Units

The school staff, counselor and members of the Aboriginal community jointly developed a program in a rural primary school in New South Wales. Support for it was obtained from all sections of the school community. The unit of study included: books written by and about Aborigines and their way of life; traditional learning methods, family roles and rights; arts and crafts; Aboriginal history of the local area, excursions to Aboriginal settlement areas and sacred sites. Local Aboriginal leaders visited the school to assist with the project.

In South Australia, several projects for Aboriginal students have been written up in the pages of the DSP journal *Priority One*. Port Augusta Primary School in 1977 began an Aboriginal language elective and children heard songs and stories from Aboriginal elders. In 1980 language courses were begun in the High School. Excursions to learn traditional bush skills accompanied the language programs. The learning difficulties for non-urban Aborigines arriving at the school are recognized as requiring teacher inservice and sensitivity, changes in teaching strategies and ways of relating to these children.

5. Whole-School Planning — Trial Of A Model

This project was funded by the New South Wales DSP in 1986 and a full report was received by the State Committee in 1987. A summary of the main features of the model was written for distribution to Regional DSP committees and secondary schools on the Disadvantaged Schools list.

The process followed by the school involved an awareness-raising discussion period after which a broad question about desired curriculum change was put to the whole school community, parents, teachers and students. The 44 separate items received in response were then submitted to the school community using the Delphi technique to establish the top priority. Visits were made to other schools working in the same problem area, followed by the development of a school solution through many workshops and meetings. A clear action plan was decided upon for 1987.

At the same time another high priority area was pursued, 'curriculum provision and choice,' although no definite action plan emerged from this more complex area by the end of the year. The time frame for the project was too short considering the large number of meetings required and the work involved in sifting the responses in the Delphi process. It also became clear that the parents needed more preliminary information about the school and the constraints on curriculum change before they could participate fully in such a model.

Notes

Chapter 1. Social Justice in Education

1. Figure kindly supplied by Toronto Board of Education Research Department.
2. R.W. Connell, K.M. Johnston and V.M.White, *Measuring Up: Assessment, Evaluation and Educational Disadvantage*, Canberra, Australian Curriculum Studies Association, 1992, p.80.
3. P. Anisef, *Accessibility to Postsecondary Education in Canada*, Education Support Branch, Department of the Secretary of State of Canada, 1985, pp.115–16. Strictly speaking the census figures are those 'at home with at least some university'. Anisef's report has an extensive discussion of the problems of measurement in these issues.
4. A. Dilmot, 'From most to least', *Australian Society*, 1990, vol. 9 no. 7, pp.14–17.
5. M. Walzer, *Spheres of Justice*, New York, Basic Books, 1983.
6. J. Rawls, *A Theory of Justice*, Cambridge MA, Harvard University Press, 1971.
7. L.T. Hobhouse, *The Elements of Social Justice*, London, George Allen and Unwin, 1922, p.107.
8. For general surveys of these issues in Australian education see the special issue 'Social Justice and Education', ed. F.Rizvi, *Discourse*, vol. 11 no. 1, 1990; and R.Lingard, J.Knight and P.Porter, ed., *Schooling Reform in Hard Times*, London, Falmer, forthcoming.
9. Department of Employment, Education and Training, *A Fair Chance for All*, Canberra, DEET, 1990.
10. R.W. Connell, D.J.Ashenden, S.Kessler and G.W.Dowsett, *Making the Difference: Schools, Families and Social Division*, Sydney, Allen and Unwin, 1982.
11. See the excellent review of this research, and its troubled relationship with educational practice, in G.Whitty, *Sociology and School Knowledge*, London, Methuen, 1985.

Chapter 2. Poverty and Compensatory Education

1. M. Lipton, *Why Poor People Stay Poor*, London, Temple Smith, 1977, shows the specificity of rural poverty. The explosive growth of third-world cities since Lipton wrote does not obliterate the difference, but gives more importance to what I have called 'Poverty 2'. W.Sachs, 'Development: a guide to the ruins', *New Internationalist* no. 232, 1992, rightly cautions against equating a frugal nonwestern economic life with 'poverty': it is the *destruction* of frugal cultures by colonialism, post-colonial states, and the global economy, that produces mass deprivation.

2. P. Freire, *Pedagogy of the Oppressed*, New York, Continuum, 1970.

3. O. Lewis, *Five Families: Mexican Case Studies in the Culture of Poverty*, New York, Basic Books, 1959.

4. US Bureau of the Census, *Statistical Abstract of the United States: 1991*, 11th edition, Washington D.C., 1991.

5. J. Dewey, *Democracy and Education*, New York, Macmillan, 1916.

6. Not entirely a joke. That *was* done with Aboriginal children in Australia up to the 1950s.

7. For the intellectual history see M.B. Katz, *The Undeserving Poor*, New York, Pantheon, 1989; and J.R. Jeffrey, *Education for Children of the Poor*, Columbus, Ohio State University Press, 1978.

8. For examples of these gradients see the research summarized in R.W. Connell, V.M. White and K.M. Johnston, *Running Twice as Hard*, Geelong, Deakin University Press, 1991.

9. C. Jencks and P.E. Peterson, ed., *The Urban Underclass*, Washington, Brookings Institution, 1991.

10. For details see chapter 2 of Connell, White and Johnston, *Running Twice as Hard*.

11. D.P. Doyle and B.S. Cooper, ed., *Federal Aid to the Disadvantaged: What Future for Chapter 1?*, London, Falmer, 1988, is a useful guide to technocratic thinking in compensatory education.

12. J. Kozol, *Savage Inequalities: Children in America's Schools*, New York, Crown, 1991.

13. L. Walker, *Australian Maid*, PhD Thesis in Sociology, Macquarie University, 1989.

14. M. Fine, *Framing Dropouts*, Albany, State University of New York Press, 1991.

15. R.W. Connell, 'Cool guys, swots and wimps: the interplay of masculinity and education', *Oxford Review of Education*, 1989, vol. 15 no. 3, 291–303.

16. I. Goodson, ed., *Social Histories of Secondary Curriculum*, London, Falmer, 1985; I. Goodson, *The Making of Curriculum*, London, Falmer, 1988.

17. P. Bourdieu and J.-C. Passeron, *Reproduction in Education, Society and Culture*, trans R. Nice, London, Sage, 1977; S. Bowles and H. Gintis, *Schooling in Capitalist America*, New York, Basic Books, 1976.

18. As argued by D. Smith, *The Everyday World as Problematic*, Toronto, University of Toronto Press, 1987, chapter 5.

19. Catherine E. Snow, et al., *Unfulfilled Expectations: Home and School Influences on Literacy*, Cambridge MA, Harvard University Press, 1991, is a useful recent example of such research, clearly showing the limits of an individualist understanding of the issues, and the power of the collective situation in determining the (depressing) outcomes.

20. Bourdieu and Passeron, *Reproduction*.

21. Connell, Ashenden, Kessler and Dowsett, *Making the Difference*; compare P.W. Cookson Jr. and C.H. Hodges, *Preparing for Power: America's Elite Boarding Schools*, New York, Basic Books, 1985.

Chapter 3: Knowledge and Society

1. For example, A.Hamilton, *Nature and Nurture: Aboriginal Child-Rearing in North-Central Arnhem Land*, Canberra, Australian Institute of Aboriginal Studies, 1981.

2. T.Kuhn, *The Structure of Scientific Revolutions*, Chicago, University of Chicago Press, 1970.

3. S. Harding, *The Science Question in Feminism*, Ithaca, Cornell University Press, 1986; E.F.Keller, *Reflections on Gender and Science*, New Haven, Yale University Press, 1985; B.Ehrenreich and D.English, *For Her Own Good*, New York, Anchor, 1989 [1978].

4. I. Goodson, ed., *Social Histories of Secondary Curriculum*, London, Falmer, 1985.

5. R.W. Connell, *Teachers' Work*, Sydney, Allen and Unwin, 1985; M.Apple, *Teachers and Texts*, New York, Routledge and Kegan Paul, 1986.

6. E. Clarke, *Assessment in Queensland Secondary Schools...1964–1983*, Brisbane, Department of Education, 1987; E.Clarke, *Assessment in Queensland Secondary Schools...1983–1990*, Brisbane, Department of Education, 1990; W.F.Connell, *Remaking Australian Education 1960–1985*, Melbourne, Australian Council for Educational Research, 1992.

7. *Australian Teacher* advertising insert, 1990.

8. S. Delamont, *Knowledgeable Women: Structuralism and the Reproduction of Elites*, London, Routledge, 1989.

9. See the feminist teachers discussed in my *Teachers' Work*, and the

working-class boys discussed in 'Cool guys...'.

10. I have in mind especially Bourdieu's concept of the 'cultural arbitrary' in Bourdieu and Passeron, *Reproduction*.

11. In addition to the references in note 3 above, see C. Merchant, *The Death of Nature*, San Francisco, Harper and Row, 1983, and B. Easlea, *Science and Sexual Oppression*, London, Weidenfeld and Nicolson, 1981.

12. R.W. Connell, 'The big picture: masculinities in recent world history', *Theory and Society*, forthcoming.

13. A. Jakubowicz, 'The celebration of (moderate) diversity in a racist society: multiculturalism and education in Australia', *Discourse*, 1988, vol. 8 no. 2.

14. M. Deutscher, *Subjecting and Objecting*, Brisbane, University of Queensland Press, 1983.

15. A useful survey of the classic sociology of knowledge is P. Hamilton, *Knowledge and Social Structure*, London, Routledge and Kegan Paul, 1974.

16. G.Lukacs, *History and Class Consciousness*, London, Merlin, 1971.

17. As I have argued in R.W.Connell, *Gender and Power*, Stanford, Stanford University Press, 1987.

Chapter 4. Curricular Justice

1. M. Walzer, 'Justice here and now', in F.S. Lucash, ed., *Justice and Equality Here and Now*, Ithaca, Cornell University Press, 1986.

2. Australian Education Council, *Hobart Declaration on Schooling: Common and Agreed National Goals for Schooling in Australia*, Hobart, AEC, 1989.

3. For the history of this issue see C. Pateman, *The Sexual Contract*, Stanford, Stanford University Press, 1988.

4. J. Blackburn et al., *Ministerial Review of Postcompulsory Schooling*, Melbourne, Department of Education, 1985; D. Ashenden, J. Blackburn, W.Hannan and D.White, 'Manifesto for a democratic curriculum', *Australian Teacher*, no. 7, 1984, pp.13–20.

5. C. Duke, 'Australian education aid — who benefits?', in P. Eldridge, D. Forbes and D. Porter, ed., *Australian Overseas Aid: Future Directions*, Sydney, Croom Helm, 1986, pp.133–148.

6. See Connell, Johnston and White, *Measuring Up*.

7. Connell, *Teachers' Work*, p.17.

8. M. Messner and D. Sabo, ed., *Sport, Men and the Gender Order*, Cham-

paign, Human Kinetics Books, 1990.

9. H.L. Gates, Jr., *Loose Canons: Notes on the Culture Wars*, New York, Oxford University Press, 1992; J.Brett, 'Literature and politics', reprinted in J. Lee et al., ed., *The Temperament of Generations*, Melbourne, Meanjin and Melbourne University Press, 1990.

10. R. Sharp and J. O'Leary, 'Independent working cless education: a repressed historical alternative', *Discourse*, 1989, vol. 10 no. 1.

11. G. Bowles and R. Duelli, ed., *Theories of Women's Studies*, Boston, Routledge and Kegan Paul, 1983; J.Aaron and S.Walby, *Out of the Margins: Women's Studies in the Ninetias*, London, Falmei, 1991.

12. T.Roszak, *The Cult of Information*, London, Paladin, 1988, ch.7.

13. Commonwealth Schools Commission, *Quality and Equality*, Canberra, CSC, 1985, p.98.

14. Cluster Productions, *Hands On: The Computing Kit*, Erskineville, DSP Centre, c.1988; C. Ryan and V. Davy, *The Essential Curriculum Project, Progress Report to December 1989*, Sydney, Disadvantaged Schools Program Metropolitan East Region, 1990.

Chapter 5. Work for Teachers

1. For an introduction to this research see T. Seddon and R.W. Connell, 'Teachers' work', *International Encyclopaedia of Education*, Supplementary Volume I, Sydney, Pergamon Press, 1989, pp.740–744. This chapter draws on the approach outlined there, and on chapters 6 and 9 of Connell, *Teachers' Work*.

2. Quoted in Connell, *Teachers' Work*, p.70.

3. M.W. Apple and K. Teitelbaum, 'Are teachers losing control of their skills and the curriculum?' *Journal of Curriculum Studies*, 1986, vol. 18, pp.177–184; M. Apple, *Teachers and Texts: A Political Economy of Class and Gender Relations in Education*, New York, Routledge and Kegan Paul, 1986.

4. See 'Teaching and the emotions', *Teachers' Work*, pp.115–125.

5. R.W. Connell, 'The workforce of reform', *Australian Journal of Education*, 1991, vol.35 no.3, pp.229–245, and Connell, White and Johnston, *Running Twice as Hard*.

6. T. Seddon, 'Teachers' work and political action', in T. Husen and N. Postlethwaite, ed., *International Encyclopaedia of Educational Research*, Pergamon, forthcoming.

7. A. Yeatman, *Bureaucrats, Technocrats, Femocrats*, Sydney, Allen and Unwin, 1990; M. Pusey, *Economic Rationalism in Canberra*, London, Cambridge University Press, 1991.

Chapter 6. Assessment

1. For discussion of these terms see Connell, Johnston and White, *Measuring Up*, chapter 2, and Y. Wadsworth, *Everyday Evaluation on the Run*, Melbourne, Action Research Issues Association, 1991.

2. For background on evaluation models see G.F. Madaus, M. Scriven and D.L. Stufflebeam, *Evaluation Models*, Boston, Kluwer-Nijhoff, 1983, and P. Broadfoot, ed., *Selection, Certification and Control*, London, Falmer, 1984.

3. G.W. Dowsett et al., 'Divisively to school: some evidence on class, sex and education in the 1940s and 1950s', *Australia 1939–1988, A Bicentennial History Bulletin*, no.4, 1981, pp.32–60.

4. Inner London Education Authority, *The London Record of Achievement: Putting Students First*, London, ILEA, 1989.

5. Quoted in Connell, Johnston and White, *Measuring Up*, p.45.

6. S. Leacock, *My Discovery of England*, Dodd, Mead & Co., 1922.

7. As indicated, long ago, by commentators such as J. McV. Hunt, *Intelligence and Experience*, New York, Ronald Press, 1961.

Chapter 7. Learning from Experience: The Disadvantaged Schools Program

1. R.W. Connell, V. White and K. Johnston, 'Poverty and education: changing conceptions', *Discourse*, 1990, vol. 11 no. 1, pp.5–20.

2. T. Roper, *The Myth of Equality*, Melbourne, National Union of Australian University Students, 1970; Committee of Enquiry into Education in South Australia, *Education in South Australia*, Adelaide, 1971.

3. J. Blackburn, *Policy Ideas in the Disadvantaged Schools Program*, paper prepared for Department of Employment, Education and Training, 1989.

4. P. Harris, *Child Poverty, Inequality and Social Justice*, Melbourne, Brotherhood of St. Laurence, 1989.

5. S. Kemmis and F. Rizvi, *Dilemmas of Reform: An Overview of Issues and Achievements of the Participation and Equity Program in Victorian Schools 1984–1986*, Geelong, Deakin University Press, 1987.

6. A. Ruby et al., *Report of the National Review of the Disadvantaged Schools Program*, Commonwealth Schools Commission, Canberra, 1985; Quality of Education Review Committee, *Quality of Education in Australia*, Canberra, Australian Government Publishing Service, 1985; Commonwealth Schools Commission, *Quality and Equality*, Canberra, 1985.

7. Commonwealth Government of Australia, *Towards a Fairer Australia: Social Justice under Labor*, Canberra, Australian Government Publishing Service, 1988; Social Justice Unit, Department of Premier and Cabinet, *South Australia's Social Justice Strategy: Building a Brighter Future*, Adelaide, 1989.

8. K.N. Ross, S. Farish and K. French, *The Development and Application of Indicators of Educational Disadvantage. Based on Census Description of the Neighbourhoods Associated with Australian Schools*, Canberra, Commonwealth Schools Commission, 1985; I. Manning, *Disadvantaged Schools Program: A Further Review of the Index of Disadvantage*, Canberra, National Institute of Economic and Industry Research, 1986.

9. W. Hannah, 'Some reflections on the concept of educational disadvantage', in I. Palmer, ed., *Melbourne Studies in Education 1985*, Melbourne, Melbourne University Press, pp.74-116.

10. Blackburn, *Policy Ideas*.

11. P.W. Musgrave, *Society and the Curriculum in Australia*, Sydney, Allen and Unwin, 1979; Connell, *Remaking Australian Education*.

12. For instance Connell, Ashenden, Kessler and Dowsett, *Making the Difference*, chapter 5.

13. For instance the 'Australian Council for Educational Standards', which published a *Review* containing articles on topics like 'The importance of rigour'.

14. For instance the Essential Curriculum Project in NSW, mentioned in Chapter 4 above.

15. For instance J.Kenway, *Public Education and Social Change: Whose Agenda?*, keynote address to Annual Conference of the Federation of Parents and Citizens Associations of NSW, Sydney, 1989.

Chapter 8. Work for Researchers

1. M. Foucault, *Discipline and Punish*, New York, Pantheon, 1977; Keller, *Reflections*; S. Bordo, *The Flight to Objectivity*, State University of New York Press, 1987.

2. Yeatman, *Bureaucrats*; Pusey, *Economic Rationalism*.

3. Y. Wadsworth, *Do It Yourself Social Research*, Melbourne, Victorian Council of Social Service and Allen and Unwin, 1983; Y. Wadsworth, *Everyday Evaluation on the Run*, Melbourne, Action Research Issues Association, 1991.

4. Among many sources of this argument see J. Dewey, *Democracy and Education*, New York, Macmillan, 1916; K. Popper, *The Logic of Scientific Discovery*, New York, Basic Books, 1959; J. Habermas, *Knowl-*

edge and Human Interests, Boston, Beacon, 1971.

5. R.W. Connell, 'AIDS: The "Social Aspects of Prevention of AIDS" (SAPA) Project', in J. Daly and E. Willis, ed., *The Social Sciences and Health Research*, Public Health Association of Australia, 1990, pp. 27–32; G. Dowsett, M. Davis and R. Connell, 'Gay men, HIV/AIDS and social research: an antipodean perspective', in P. Aggleton, P. Davies and G. Hart, ed., *AIDS: Rights, Risk and Reason*, London, Falmer, 1992, pp.1–12.